Mental Toughness

A Step by Step Guide to Master Your Mind, Boost Your Will Power and Achieve Your Goals

Rahim Abdul

from various sources. Please consult a licensed professional before attempting any techniques outlined in this book.

By reading this document, the reader agrees that under no circumstances is the author responsible for any losses, direct or indirect, that are incurred as a result of the use of the information contained within this document, including, but not limited to, errors, omissions, or inaccuracies.

Table of Contents

Introduction

"The strength of your mind determines the quality of your life." - Edmond Mbiaka

Most people have, at one point in our lives, complained about how our lives are jeopardized by things that are beyond our control. What about the things that are? Why is it that we still complain about things that we know we can control? Why is it that people spend a good part of their lives and are still unable to introduce discipline in life, fight off mood swings, and control their stress?

For the longest part of my life, I have seen many people from all walks of life struggling to find the kind of mental strength they need to make things work for them. There is no denying that we all wish to be successful in whatever we choose to do, but how many actually end up being successful?

Of course, the answer to this question isn't simple, especially considering the fact that all of us hold a unique perspective and definition on what success means to us individually. However, there are some uniformities. Most of us believe success is having enough money in the bank, a lavish lifestyle, and that all worries automatically fade with little effort. If that is the case, Jim Carrey, a renowned Hollywood Superstar countered the argument and quoted:

"I think everybody should get rich and famous and do everything they ever dreamed of so they can see that's not the answer."

Clearly, making a lot of money didn't work for him. Then, what is that aspect that manages to evade us? What is it that we are missing in life that could help us actually be on top of our game, do what we please, and become great leaders, entrepreneurs, business professionals and better people? The answer is mental toughness.

While the world continues to turn every stone and find their success, they often overlook the importance of having mental toughness. By that, I do not mean that one should act stubborn, rude and bully others. Mental toughness is a skill that allows anyone the ability to do things in life that are otherwise perceived as impossible or too difficult.

I could go on writing a book about 25 great ideas to make money from in the coming years, or how to fight procrastination, and they would do fine, but at the root of everything lies your mental toughness. If you have the mental capacity to endure tough situations, handle pressure, stress and manage anxiety at will, there is absolutely nothing that can stop you from achieving your goals and go further than what you thought was possible. However, the reality is that we are far too often caught up with all of these.

You may have a seven-figure bank account, and yet you will not be at ease. The longer that happens, the more you start taking a U-turn in life. Piece by piece, everything will come crashing down.

Mental toughness is what can get you to fight against stress, depression, anxiety, and a lot more. It is what can allow you to have a good night's sleep. Through it, you can get to make bold and meaningful decisions in life, and enjoy healthy relationships. It is through mental toughness that you will be able to become honest with yourself, explore, identify and acknowledge your weaknesses and then work on them.

"To rectify a problem, one must acknowledge that there is one."

Every problem can be solved, and each of these problems requires you to have some level of mental toughness. Imagine the kind of life you can start living if you gain enough mental toughness to outlast all challenges of life and solve problems with ease as they come. This is what this book aims to do, teach you exactly how to unlock your mental toughness. If you are tired of being upset, if you are tired of being stressed out and have no idea where to turn to, let me help you rediscover your rhythm once again. Allow me to teach you how to become a true success story, one that may go on to inspire and teach many others in life.

There are so many things in life that we often overlook not because we do not know about them, but because no one came up to us and told us how important of a role they go on to play. Sure enough, mental toughness is one of them. Take note of whether you experience any of the following. If so, practicing the given exercises in this book will help you strengthen your mind.

- Stressed out everyday
- Losing or lacking willpower
- Inability to pursue what you want
- Feeling clueless or lost
- Losing temper for no obvious reasons
- Forgetting details
- Irregular sleeping patterns
- Feeling tired or exhausted even after hours of sleep
- Loss of appetite or eating far too much

These are some of the symptoms that go on to suggest something is terribly wrong. If you can relate to any of this, stop treating it lightly. Leave these symptoms or problems unattended and things will only get worse. The best way forward is to take the first step and the best time to do that is now.

Why This Book?

There are hundreds of thousands of self-help books out there. Each of these packed with information that may or may not provide you with the answers you are looking for. While one may have good facts, they may not provide you with solutions or techniques to use and adopt as a part of your daily routines. Then, there are books that go on to talk all about techniques that one would need a specialized degree to understand. All of this often ends up in a massive disaster for the readers.

I have read quite a few myself and I say this from experience. A good self-help book is one that uses the simplest of languages and explains theories and techniques well. This is why I decided to put together all of my ideas, research, facts, theories and exercises in one place without using any daunting words that may otherwise intimidate readers who may not be so fond of technical terminologies.

Obviously, writing a book means that one must think matters through. There is no point in writing something that claims to teach you something and fails to do so by the end of it. To ensure that does not happen, I will divide this book into two major sections. The first one will introduce you to all kinds of facts and theories along with relevant examples to further explain concepts and allow you, the readers, a thorough understanding. The other part of the book will focus more on practical techniques that I will be talking about. To me, it is essential that you not only gain knowledge, but also get to apply the same right away.

We will be covering quite a few things, all pertaining to mental toughness. To give you a taste of what we we will be learning within this book, here is a list of things I will be talking about:

- Mental toughness - We will learn exactly what I mean by mental toughness. We will explore all about mental toughness, what it is, why it is important, and what can it do for you.

- Weak mind - I will talk in great detail of what a weak mind is and how you can go on to gain mental toughness. Of course, most of us may not know we have a weak mind which is why I will explain how you can find out if you have one.

- Common traps to avoid - There are far too many things people end up getting wrong. I will ensure that I discuss every single one of these and aware you of what you must and must not do.

- Willpower - For those who may have been looking for a way to build up a strong willpower, I will provide you with significant information on how to do just that.

- How to build mental toughness - Obviously, I cannot consider my book complete without actually talking about this. You will learn all you need to get started and build your mental toughness.

- Exercises - From "how to build mental toughness in five minutes a day" to "Ten easy steps to build mental toughness," I will share many practical exercises and examples for you to try, learn, understand and adapt.

"Why can't I just skip to the part where I learn these exercises?" Of course you can, but you will soon find that you may not understand quite a few things and concepts. You may not understand how things work or what the entire science behind these exercises is. To ensure that doesn't happen, I have organized the chapter in a way that you first gain the knowledge, so that you know what you are required to do, and then start using the second section of the book accordingly. That way, the results would not only be prominent, they'll be phenomenal.

Who Am I?

Allow me to introduce myself. My name is Rahim Abdul. I grew up as a mentally weak person, and I do not feel ashamed to admit that. In fact, had I not been that way, I would have probably never found a will within me to change my circumstances.

I was the kind of person who would forget the simplest of things. I never had any goals set up because to me, they never became a reality. I tried countless times to set up regular goals, not even tough ones, and I would instantly find myself failing right at the beginning. Needless to say, I had enough and I decided I no longer need goals as all my efforts would still fetch me failure. I had abandoned something not because I couldn't do it, but because I didn't know what I was missing at that point in time.

One fine day, while I was quite young, it dawned upon me. After reflecting much on my own self, I realized I was lacking a few things in life. It did not take long before I started learning about self-help. This new world of possibilities started opening to me, presenting me with both challenges and excitement at the same time. Sure enough, I was eager, so eager that I would practice what I learned every day. However, despite all that, I still ended up failing these exercises, and this time, it was my laziness.

I had the knowledge, but my mind was just not ready to take things up as I wanted it to. This is where I heard the phrase "mental toughness" and I knew that's what I was missing. I had no idea what made me say that, but I started researching as much as I could. For months, I gathered significant facts, data, theories and exercises, all of which I started to practice. I learned all the fundamentals involved. I picked up numerous techniques and I gave each of these a shot. During this phase of experimenting, I learned many things, including my absolute favorite technique - meditation. While other techniques changed some aspects, meditation had the biggest impact on my life. It transformed me into a new, more confident, more mentally tough person. I was no longer enslaved to depression, stress, or anxiety. From that day, I continue to exercise these techniques and lead a much, much better life than I could have ever imagined.

Since *Mental Toughness* is my way to help you unlock your mental toughness, I will share all of these techniques, tips and tricks so that you too can experience these significant changes firsthand. There is no point in just reading about how good these are and visualize what kind of impact they may bring to your life. Through this book, I will guide you with a step-by-step approach, just to ensure that anyone who may have never picked up a self-help book before knows exactly what needs to be done. If you are someone who has experienced such aspects, you too will find valuable information within this book. With that said, it is time to gear up, set aside the mountain of stress and worries, and begin your journey to unlock what can very possibly be the biggest turning point in your life.

Side note: This book will specifically talk about mental toughness and aspects related to the subject alone. Anything outside of the scope is neither discussed nor covered within the book. For best results, practice techniques on a daily basis and allow yourself some time with them to experience results.

Chapter 1

Understanding Mental Toughness and Mental Toughness Mindset

Our journey to fully understand mental toughness and harness the fringe benefits it has to offer begins by addressing the definition of mental toughness.

It took me a long time before I understood what mental toughness is. In this chapter, you can expect to learn:

- A working definition of mental toughness
- The mental toughness mindset
- How this differs from things such as resilience, motivation, et cetera
- What these work best with

Mental Toughness - 101

If you are someone who has a bit of a background in psychology, you might already have an idea what mental toughness is. However, since there are many who may not know, mental toughness is an ability that allows a person to resist, manage, and even overcome doubts, concerns, worries, among other things. It is something that allows you to overcome circumstances that would normally block or prevent you from experiencing success, excelling as tasks, or moving towards your goals that you may have set (Mental Toughness Inc., n.d.).

There was a time in my life where I had all the goals lined up, but I did not have the vehicle that could take me from here to there. Mental toughness is your vehicle that will grant you the ability to do a lot more in life without worrying about tough situations, decision-making processes, and all the stress that may come your way.

The term itself is widely used in sports psychology. The academic definition may sound a bit boring, but it is one that we should learn, to further develop a better understanding of this fine ability. The definition states:

"Having the natural or developed psychological edge that enables you to: generally, cope better than your opponents with the many demands (competition, training, lifestyle) that sport places on a performer;

specifically, be more consistent and better than your opponents in remaining determined, focused, confident, and in control under pressure." (Jones, 2002).

Mental toughness is a skill set that anyone can learn and acquire. It is something that can be improved with time, provided that one continues to practice and apply the knowledge in real-life scenarios and situations. It can also be applied and used in all areas of life.

Whether you are a fresh graduate, a professional, a business person, or even an entrepreneur in the making, having mental toughness allows you to train yourself and own a quality lifestyle. Through the use of mental toughness, you can go on to become the most sought-after leader in the business. It is a defining trait that all leaders and people at positions of authority share in common. They use this skill to excel in all areas of life including decision-making, problem solving, leading the team, thinking out of the box, voicing out opinions, and taking charge when necessary.

With that said, the phrase "mental toughness" is quite a vast one. Within its scope, there are many aspects that one can learn.

The Mindset of a Winner

By learning mental toughness, the first and perhaps the most obvious thing anyone would notice is the presence of a new mindset, one that will take the necessary action to win. Think about yourself as a performer. Using mental toughness, you will no longer feel the need to hide behind someone or wait until someone else has a go first. You will take the lead and step ahead. Whether you go on to win or not becomes irrelevant. The mindset of a winner is what pushes you to come out of the shadows and be at the forefront, a typical trait of a leader.

You might be hung up on the part where I said it's irrelevant whether you win or lose, and you wouldn't be wrong, but let me shed a little light there. If you are an athlete, you know that your job is to go out there and give it your best shot every single time. If you win, good, but if you don't, you still get to walk away with a satisfaction that you gave it your best. That is a mindset we all need in order to be anywhere near our perceived success. Why? If we are being honest, most of us work not because we want to, but because we have to. Within those two words lies a massive difference.

Whatever we want to do, we will always do it with utmost commitment. We will not worry how hard things will become because we know that nothing will shake us off the track. That passion, commitment and drive to achieve something always produces positive results. They may not necessarily be exactly how you envisioned, but you'd still have something by the end of it. Then, you can analyze what changed and what went wrong, restart, and hit the mark the next time around.

On the other hand, let's assume we have a regular nine to five job. The pay is good too, and you get all the benefits such as quarterly bonuses, paid leaves, medical benefits, et cetera. However, despite having all that, you will start losing that commitment and passion to work just after the first month or so. I am not suggesting that you will completely lose that desire to work, but it would be more of a burden that you just have to deal with. Now, your job becomes a responsibility. Now, the same job that you were once too excited for is growing stale. See the difference? Take away the commitment and you will either end up getting fired or finding yourself a better job. Even if you continue with the same job, your mind will still not be at rest. It will still push you to search for better alternatives.

The above two examples highlight the difference as clear as night and day. One has a winner's mentality while the other doesn't. Under no circumstances am I suggesting that having a job is bad. However, that being said, if you were to introduce the winner's mindset to your job, you might be in for some treat.

Once you adopt the winner's mindset, you start performing at your best every day. When that happens at your workplace, people will start noticing the change in you. Your mentality will start producing results and creating impressions, eventually leading you to a higher rank. The best news is that the journey doesn't end there. You can still apply the same mentality and go forward, climb the success ladder higher, or even launch your own venture. The options are limitless, and it is only made possible if you choose to train your mind to have a winner's mindset. That is something that mental toughness will teach you effortlessly as you shall see later on in the book.

Hyper Focus

I once had a major problem keeping my focus on things. I was one of those who would easily get distracted by noises, people moving, cars honking their horns, and other similar stimuli. Most of us fail to realize that this isn't a good thing. If we are so easily distracted, it goes to show that we never had enough focus on the task we were preoccupied with. We'd be lying to ourselves if we say otherwise.

By learning mental toughness, you get to develop what is called hyper focus. It is a skill that allows you to have complete mental clarity, comfort, and ease. When your thought process is clear, it cannot be distracted at all. Furthermore, it takes no rocket scientist to figure out that if you cannot get distracted, you can focus on your task completely without ever worrying that something out of the blue might distract you.

You may have experienced this a lot of times too. It isn't something new because we normally call it being in the zone. Remember the last time you were focusing so deeply on your assignment that time flew right by and you did not move an inch until the job was done? At the end of the task, you felt proud of what you had accomplished. That's exactly what hyper focus is all about.

Stress Optimization

Okay, before I even go on talking about stress, let me share some alarming statistics about stress itself.

The year 2020 has been one that will go down in history as one of the darkest years of our time. It did what two massive wars couldn't, shut everything down. Of course, we all know enough about COVID-19, but have you wondered how that has affected people mentally?

Stress was already one of the leading causes of deaths in the United States. The South Louisiana Medical Associates (SLMA) stated that around 120,000 people die every year because of work-related stress (SLMA, n.d.). Mind you, this was before the rise of the horrific and deadly virus. If that wasn't enough, stress has gone on to increase far beyond anyone of us could've imagined.

The American Psychological Association (APA) suggests that nearly eight of every ten adults say that the coronavirus has gone on to significantly increase their stress levels in life (APA, 2020).

Stress is everywhere. Despite having so much technology, we are still miles away from fully understanding what stress is and how humanity can finally learn to say goodbye to it. However, it isn't all dark and gloomy. There are ways through which you can learn to manage your stress, and luckily for us, mental toughness teaches us exactly that. Through this ability, one can learn how to manage stress and pressure when performing any given task. Add to that the mental toughness itself, you stop having doubts, fear or any kind of anxiety. That means that the task will be done with optimum efficiency, dedication, and will remain completely stress-free.

By learning how to manage stress, you will also gain the ability to not bow down in the face of fear which, in other circumstances, would normally see you cave in or deter from your original task. Mastering this ability will allow you to become a better person and one that performs even in the most stressful situations.

Failing Well

Everyone fears failure, and certainly no one can say they like to fail. However, failure is a major part of success, and this is not just me trying to make you believe in that. There have been countless personalities, leaders, and entrepreneurs who have used failure as a stepping stone to learn more. Simply put, without failure, you will never truly appreciate success.

Let me paraphrase a short story originating from England. Not so long ago, a man invested his life savings into an idea that he developed on his own. He found the traditional vacuum cleaners far too complicated and the process of cleaning the bag a little too cumbersome. He decided he would change that.

He used his money to develop well over 5,000 prototypes, all of which failed. However, that did not stop him at all. He knew he was on to something big, something revolutionary. With each failing prototype, he gained more knowledge, allowing him to perfect his design before finally, he introduced to the world with "G-force" cleaner. Obviously, no market at that time would allow him to sell his product because it could potentially disturb the market dynamics. That didn't stop him and soon afterwards, he set up Dyson Ltd, a name that today is known for its groundbreaking technology. Today, Sir James Dyson is listed as the wealthiest man in Britain with an estimated value of around 16.2 billion pounds (The Times, n.d.).

Just imagine, had he given up on the first or the second, or even the 5,000th prototype, he would have said goodbye to a once in a lifetime opportunity. However, he remained strong, showed immense willpower, and did not allow stress or fear of failure dictate terms. He remained calm in the face of failure itself and kept pushing.

Learning how to take failure well allows you to do that. It lets you explore things in life that you may not dare to explore otherwise. It helps you improve your own knowledge and skills as well.

Maxing Out Limits

We all have been there and we all have experienced this as well. We often work far too much and feel completely burned out. It's just like hitting the gym and working out until your muscles are no longer able to lift even the lightest of the dumbbells. We simply call it a day and leave. The same is seen at work as well. Whether you are operating your own business or working for someone else, you have a perceived limit to which you can work. Anything beyond that is simply impossible. What if I told you there is a way you can increase that limit and go beyond.

You might think I am just making stuff up now, but I assure you it is actually possible. Our limits are not set by our bodies, but it is actually our mind that sends out signals to the rest of the body to stop. Why? Because it starts experiencing stress, pain, exhaustion and many other things. If we learn how to train our mind to endure some more physical exertion, we might just be able to work for a few more hours, be more productive, get more done and be compensated for all the extra efforts as well.

Mental toughness allows you to learn that as well. Call it a side effect, but it does get the job done, and that for now is all that we care about.

Preparedness

One of the biggest reasons for failure is lack of planning. Whether you ask someone to marry you or start a brand new business idea that you knew would work, if you do not have a plan to back you up with, you are likely to grow cold feet and walk away.

Some may argue that planning isn't exactly their forte, but then again, I never said it was mine either. However, when you start learning and experiencing mental toughness, you will gain the ability and the confidence to prepare your mind for any eventuality. That is essentially done through planning, and planning requires you to have focus, confidence, positivity and energy, all of which mental planning grants you. See how they are interconnected?

When you start working according to a plan, you will always know where you are supposed to go, what you are supposed to do and how far along you have come. Once you have a few plans in motion, you can also start working on backup plans where you analyze the situation and predict the possible future scenarios and then use that to plan your next moves. What if you were a teacher and the school was shut down? Well, you can always teach online, and that is a solution that you thought of and added in as a part of your plan. If that situation plays out, you'd know what you need to do without wasting a second of your time.

These are some of the things that I have highlighted just to show you how incredibly useful and powerful mental toughness truly is. Take it from a guy who continues to use mental toughness even after all these years. I don't do so because I like it, I do so because it has now become a part of me. Through mental toughness, I gained the clarity I needed to focus on my tasks. Through it, I gained the confidence to help others. Through mental toughness, I also gained the skill to manage stress, plan my next moves and even write this book. All of this would not have been possible had I not learned mental toughness when I did.

Diving Deeper

I mentioned earlier that mental toughness can be considered as a skill, and then I went on to highlight a few components that chip in to the entire concept. Eagle-eyed readers may have already spotted that these additional traits and skills create a kind of personality, a complete mindset. Mental toughness is exactly that; a complete mindset that allows you to cover all related aspects.

You might think that it is teaching you how to be resilient. Resilience and mental toughness are two separate ideas. The two terms are often used interchangeably. Resilience is the ability to recover from an awry situation, either completely or largely (Lyons, n.d.). It is the ability that helps you to rise back up out of an adverse situation.

To some extent, it sounds the same as mental toughness, but there is a difference. A resilient person will always face negative situations with negativity, be brought down, or find the going getting tougher and tougher. This person may create an adverse situation and then later find their way out of it. On the other hand, a person with mental toughness is one who will look for positivity even in the most negative of situations. Such a person would not be afraid to take on challenges, and may often be tempted to seek them out. They will always look on the bright side of things.

A person without optimism is resilient. Such a person would often find the road they choose to follow growing harder and harder. There may be a time where such a person would cave in or take a fall. It would be resiliency that would still allow them to get back up and continue their pursuit ahead. However, if the situation gets too tense or stressful, they may fail completely, and may not be able to recover out of it.

Somewhere in the twentieth century, Suzanne Kobasa, an American psychologist, studied some resilient managers and found that each of them responded uniquely to stress, pressure and challenges. While all of them continued to be resilient, some, however, took the situation as an opportunity. These people ended up handling the situation far better than the rest. She termed this as hardiness and proposed that this was a separate concept than resilience. Hardiness later went on to become mental toughness (Lyons, n.d.).

While the difference between the two may seem subtle, it is still a massive one, psychologically speaking. There is no denying the fact that these two are related because they certainly are, but not in the way you might imagine.

All mentally tough individuals are resilient, however not all resilient individuals are mentally tough.

Mental Toughness Mixes well

Now that you know how mental toughness is different from resilience, it would be a lot easier to explain what it works best with. There are a few things that mental toughness works extremely well with. These are:

- Self-discipline
- Habits
- Confidence

There are a lot of other elements that you can throw in the mix, but these three are my top picks. Let me explain why.

Self-Discipline

A lot of people have often asked me if mental toughness was something that boosted motivation. Yes, it does do that. However, that is not the only thing it does. It allows you to gain willpower. It helps you set things straight and make better decisions, and it does all this to allow you to create a self-discipline that can work seamlessly together with mental toughness itself. The benefits you end up getting are far beyond words can explain.

There is no denying that we often try and find ways to gain more motivation. Whether it is because we want to join a gym but just do not have the willpower to do it or it is to start a new business venture, we need mental toughness and self-discipline.

Self-discipline, for anyone who doesn't know, is the ability to correct or regulate one's own self for the sake of improvement. If you are someone who has gained a few extra pounds or started smoking and you want to bring improvement to your health you must be self-disciplined. You must be able to take remedial actions to correct the course of your life and restore good health. You must be able to accept what is wrong and do what is right that helps you to improve your physical and mental health, habits, routine activities and even your professional matters.

Let's assume I am overweight. I have mental toughness, meaning that I take every challenge readily and happily. However, just because I am mentally tough does not mean I can do everything. To improve my own state, I need both willpower, which mental toughness provides me, and a mechanism that pushes me to work out, eat healthy diets, and shed weight. For the latter, that's where I need self-discipline. If I combine the two together, the results will be significant.

Generally, your habits, whatever they may be, form the foundation of your mental belief system. It is that mental belief system that sets you apart from others. If you are someone who arrives to work late thinking that everyone else does the same, you have a mental belief system that lets you sleep for a bit longer. Your subconscious mind keeps on believing that you will not be subjected to any penalties for being late, and you'd always continue to do that. However, if you were to find the will to change that, you'd end up creating new habits, a completely new self-discipline mechanism. Now, you'd go to bed early on, rise early, and leave early, ensuring that you always arrive on time. See how that works?

Both mental toughness and self-discipline are interlinked. One feeds you with the willpower and the positivity to take on challenges while the other allows you to define your own mechanism that helps you create that change.

Confidence

Being mentally tough does not guarantee nor grant you confidence. You may have the optimism that it brings, and you may have self-discipline, but if you lack the confidence, you will still find yourself stuck in pretty much the same situation. You need confidence to even take your first step towards your goals.

It goes without saying that confidence goes a long way to serve you in life. Whether it is to initiate a dialogue with someone you are interested in, voice out your opinions during a meeting, or even respond to a question effectively, you need confidence.

With that said, if you were to add together both confidence and mental toughness, imagine the kind of success you can fetch for yourself. You will virtually be a force to be reckoned with. Whatever you sight your sights on, you'd have the mental toughness to take on challenges in a positive manner, and have the confidence to address tough situations, take bold initiatives, and represent your image, personality and brand in ways inconceivable to you previously. If it was up to me, I would share this dynamic duo with everyone and ensure they get to experience their life changing right before their eyes. Unfortunately, I can only talk about it and try to teach you. Acting on this knowledge is completely your call.

What it Takes to be Mentally Tough

You do not have to be significantly courageous, highly intelligent, or even vastly talented. All you need is something called consistency. Yes, we all know what that is, and surprisingly enough, we all tend to overlook how important consistency is in our lives.

It is through consistency that you can go on to create a habit. It is through developing good habits that you set yourself a discipline. Consistency isn't just about habits either. For anyone who aspires to excel as an entrepreneur, a leader or a figure of authority, you need consistency. If you perform good the first day, make sure you carry the momentum forward. There is never a room for taking things easy if you truly wish to go on and create the kind of success you desire. It is through consistency that you will eventually hit your target just like Sir James Dyson did.

Mentally tough people are known to develop their own system through which they are better able to focus on all things important. They simply do not care of the number of obstacles, challenges, or hardships that may come in their way. Once they have set their sights on a goal, they will move mountains if they have to just to go on and achieve these goals. This never-ending desire and passion for success is only possible through consistency on all levels.

Consistency is vital for anyone and everyone, especially if you are trying to develop mental toughness. You cannot expect to gain mental toughness in a single day or through a single fifteen minute meditation session. This is a lifelong process. It requires and demands that you give it time every single day for the rest of your life for it to fully provide you with the benefits, joys, and success you seek. This may be a bit daunting, but I assure you, after the first few months of consistency, it will become a second nature. Things will start happening on their own because now, your subconscious knows what the intention is and what needs to be done. Don't believe me? Recall your last drive home. How many pedestrians did you see? Do you remember the drive vividly? Chances are that you don't. That is because your subconscious mind was busy getting the job done. Driving, because of the consistency, became a second nature. You may not be able to recall how many sets of traffic lights you encountered or when you flicked the indicator switch on. That was done automatically for you by you.

Using the same principle, if you create certain routines and habits and continue to use them every single day, soon, you will find your day incomplete without them. If you were to work hard and bring 100% of your commitment to the table for the next four months, I bet you that you will never be able to settle for anything less than 100% of the goal as acceptable, and you will ensure you get the job done.

Mental toughness, in the end, gets all of this done. Hopefully by now, you have a good idea of just how incredibly powerful mental toughness can be. Consider this chapter as just an introductory one because we have barely scratched the surface. There is a lot more that needs to be learned.

In the next chapter, we will look into how someone can transform a weak mind to one that is mentally tough. We will also learn how to find out if we have a weak mind. A lot of exciting information awaits us ahead.

Chapter 2:

From Weak Mind to

Mentally Tough

Our mental state is directly responsible for how we view ourselves. If we are mentally tough, we will not hesitate to ask difficult questions to ourselves. We will not back away or find excuses to not accept our errors. We will seek out such weak spots and try to improve upon them with time and experience.

Since you have learned in the previous chapter what mental toughness is, I am confident that you are now able to do this part more easily. Now that you have an open mind about mental toughness, digesting newer information would automatically become easier.

In this chapter, I not only intend to teach you how you can improve your mental state from weak to mentally tough, but I will also share with you something that I personally use to check on my mental toughness every now and then. Throughout the chapter, you will learn things like:

- Measuring your mental toughness
- Understanding what a weak mind is
- Things that negatively affect your mental toughness
- Countering the negative effects and improving mental toughness

With that said, it is time for us to move forward and learn how to figure out how mentally tough we truly are. Once we learn that, we will then move on to see how we can transform ourselves from a person with a weak mind to a person with a mentally tough one.

Gauging Mental Toughness

This may come to many as a bit of a surprise, but there is no specific way to measure mental toughness. If you search online, you will come across hundreds of ways that claim to measure your mental toughness, but none of them can guarantee 100% accurate results. There are far too many variables involved in the mix, and quite often, you might find varying results.

This, of course, is a bit of a problem for us. After all, we are trying to find out if we have the kind of mental toughness we need to go out there and claim our rightful success or not. Fortunately, there are two ways I have used myself to figure out my own mental toughness and get a decent idea of those around me as well.

The first one is quite a lengthy one. It requires you to spend around fifteen minutes of your time to complete an online psychometric measure called MTQ48. It is developed by Professor Peter Clough. It uses four main components to make up the entire test but gives you arguably the most accurate results. The four components involved within the tests are:

- Control
- Commitment
- Challenge
- Confidence

I know, this one sounds a bit boring and it seems to take forever. However, if you are looking to obtain the most accurate results, it cannot get any better than this. Trust me, if there was a better way, I would be talking about that right now.

The second method that I mentioned is actually drawn from the first one. However, in order to use the second method, which is essentially using the power of honest, impartial and unbiased observation, you must establish a good understanding of the four core components mentioned above.

Control

This is pretty self-explanatory. There are those who live to retain control on life and everything related to it and then there are those who are often controlled by others. In either case, there is always some control that one always retains.

Control is essentially having a clear sense of self-worth. This core component goes on to describe the extent to which a person feels they are in control of circumstances and life itself. This also includes how much a person can control their display of emotions (Mental Toughness Partners, n.d.).

Anyone who is mentally tough would always have a mentality conducive to moving forward regardless of how they may feel. If you recall from our earlier chapter, they have this incredible ability to add positive feelings to the mixture, allowing them to continue controlling most of the variables of a situation, if not all.

Commitment

People often set out goals, but most of them lack the commitment needed to go on and pursue those goals and bring them to fruition. This is a widespread problem, and it isn't just limited to a specific gender, age or profession. Almost everyone faces this. This component, therefore, describes just how committed a person is to set goals and seek them out. It describes the will of a person and whether this person is willing to put in the hard work needed to accomplish their goals and objectives.

A lot of people often end up combining commitment and control whenever they seek out resilience. However, it is to be noted that resilience is a passive quality. It is still a part of mental toughness, but misses out on positivity.

Challenge

Every now and then, we end up facing new situations, challenges, problems and scenarios that need us to step outside our comfort zones. Not a lot of people are able to do that. If anything, most would try and find a way around the challenging situation as opposed to going right through it. This component is used to analyze how willing a person is to accept the challenge, take risks, and push back their boundaries just to explore possible solutions and gain something relevant out of the challenging situation.

Once again, those who are mentally tough view challenges as opportunities to learn and gain. They will do whatever it takes to relish the chance and go on to increase their experience and knowledge by tackling the unknown situation. There are those who may actually enjoy seeking out challenges, and these are the ones reflected by a higher challenge score (part of MT48).

Confidence

We already looked into what confidence is and how important it is for pretty much any aspect of life. It is through confidence that a person is able to create a self-belief. The stronger the self-belief, the easier it will be for these people to make tough decisions because they would always know they can get the job done. They will also be the first ones to stand their grounds and will pretty much be unshakeable.

Remember the second way of measuring mental toughness? Now, you can observe people and start finding out how they perform in each of these categories. By doing so, you will be able to gauge the mental toughness of a person to some extent. If, for any reason, you need to get accurate scores, use the MT48 method (available throughout the internet) as that will be able to provide you with significant details about a person. This is also something that some firms use when screening potential candidates to ensure that they hire people who can take full responsibility for their actions, stand their ground when needed, and be willing to work in demanding situations.

Weak Minds

Let us imagine Peter, a thirty-year-old professional. He works a regular nine to five job, has a decent pay, and lives a decent lifestyle. However, despite that, Peter often complains how his life has come to a halt. After being suggested by a friend, Peter decides to do a self analysis and see how mentally tough he is. The scores show a grim sign. It shows that he isn't as mentally tough as he may have thought. What he possesses is a weak mind.

There are many out there, just like Peter, who do everything right by the book, but still have a weak mind. However, there is no point in being ashamed about it. If there is a will to improve, there is always a way.

You might be wondering why a person should go through all this just to improve their mind. It is a valid question, and it is one that I once had in my life. The answer is simple - we need mental toughness in all aspects of life.

A lot of people interpret mental toughness as something only the entrepreneurs or leaders need. While they aren't completely wrong, the fact is that even an average person with an average lifestyle and job would also need mental toughness. It is through mental toughness that a person would not only perform better at work, but they will also be able to experience improvement in all areas of life, such as marriage and relationships.

So what makes a person to lose mental toughness and develop a weaker mindset?

Mental toughness exists as long as you maintain consistency and develop an effective self-discipline coupled with good habits. Take any of that away and you essentially choose to undo all the hard work. To learn how to avoid that, we must find out what exactly causes a person to lose mental toughness. Once we identify these aspects, we can then learn how to overcome or avoid these.

Lack of Self-Discipline

One of the biggest reasons why we end up losing mental toughness, or not gaining one, is because of a lack of self-discipline. There are far too many activities that we either do or avoid, without knowing just how much damage these may be doing to us. Things such as sleeping on odd times or for longer durations, waking up late, munching on junk food, drinking, smoking, lying, being lazy, all of these go on to affect us, our personalities and our lifestyles.

When you lack self-discipline in life, it is fairly easy to lose confidence and the mental capacity you need to gain and retain mental toughness. You lose the ability to focus on tasks and will start finding yourself distracted rather quickly. You will start making more mistakes and you will not put in the efforts to learn from your mistakes and improve upon yourself. In simpler words, you will develop a lax mindset where whatever is going on in life is okay with you. That is essentially losing your control upon life and surrendering yourself to time.

Entrepreneurs, or people who may be thinking of becoming one, pay special attention; if you can allow such activities to dictate your term, don't start unless you have addressed these first or you will start only to find that you will fail.

Losing Confidence

Failure has a funny way of teaching us valuable lessons. What's even funnier is how we end up accepting failure. Some of us take things positively, learn from failure, and move on. However, that is not the story for us all. Most of us are actually afraid of failing at anything in life. We believe that if we fail, we will let ourselves down and those around us down as well. When we enter something with such a mindset, we are essentially creating a room within our mind for fear to settle. This fear of failure, once activated upon failing, will eat away our confidence.

You may fail something as simple as a driving test, or a job interview, however, you will end up losing your confidence as well. While others go on to use their failure as an experience and come back stronger, you, on the other hand, will come back weaker with every failure that you experience. Eventually, you will be forced to give up because your subconscious belief system would push you to believe that you are bound to fail in life.

Imagine the kind of confidence you will end up losing just because you allowed fear to settle and looked at failure from the wrong perspective. Without confidence, you will never be able to deliver an impressive interview. Without it, you will never be able to talk to your customers and build healthy relationships.

Fixing the Problem

Do not worry if you felt a connection with what I said above. It probably means you have some weakness or fear that you must deal with. Everything in this world is fixable including a weak mind. To us, that is all that matters.

Fixing a weak mind requires quite a few things to be done. With that said, before we even begin to start improving our mental toughness, we must do what is essentially a ritual. No, it doesn't involve you to do anything demonic or downright crazy. All it needs is for you to promise yourself that you will do what it takes to change things around, just to get on top of your game. Make it a habit to tell yourself loudly that you are mentally tough every morning, afternoon and evening.

There is science behind that. You see, while we prioritize our conscious mind for everything, our subconscious mind is significantly more powerful than its counterpart. Remember the drive home that I discussed earlier? That is a sheer display of just how powerful your subconscious mind is. If you keep on telling yourself that you are mentally tough, your subconscious system will start believing it and then will act upon it. It will start providing you with ways that will allow you to develop confidence, become more active, and do all that is needed to move in the right direction. Of course, this does not happen overnight. Just make it a habit and you should be able to see significant results in a couple of months. From there on, just continue doing this and life will keep on getting better.

Needless to say, there is far more that needs to be done than to feed information to your subconscious belief system. To assist you to move in the right direction, I will be shedding light upon a few things that you can begin working on right now.

Motivation

When you have motivation, you have a purpose. In a professional environment, even if you have your dream job, there will be smaller tasks that appear more mundane, but are essential to the overall function of the job. With the right amount of motivation towards the end goal, you will be able to function at your best at all times.

Positive and Negative Thinking

Where there is light, there is darkness. Similarly, if you have positive thoughts, you are sure to have some negative ones as well. It is only a natural process. However, just because it is natural does not mean that you cannot change the way it works.

If you have been following the book so far, you would know that mental toughness hinges on positive thinking. However, you cannot deny the negative thoughts and resentment that will often come your way. Having negative thoughts isn't exactly bad either. While positive thoughts allow you to fill yourself with optimism, negative thoughts allow you to anticipate what is about to come your way. By doing so, you gain the ability to plan ahead of time and prepare yourself. You can then use your positivity to fill out the void and take the challenge on in a positive and constructive manner.

Kindness and Compassion

Being mentally tough never means to be insensitive, rude or harsh. That is more of a mental disorder than a quality. While many go on to believe that they need to be tough to be leaders, it is the opposite of what they need to become one.

A leader is one who is compassionate and kind towards others. Anyone in a position of authority, if this person is rude or harsh, those who follow him will no longer be able to voice their opinions or even have productive discussion. Eventually, the followers will break away and the leadership skills will come crashing down.

Treat everyone just like the way you want to be treated. While they may not remember what you said in the meeting, they will go on to remember forever how you made them feel. It is effective and it works 100% of the time. Such potential clients or people will eventually prefer you and your company over that of others.

One Step at a Time

You may have come across the term SMART goals. If you haven't, do not worry. I will explain.

We have many goals in life, some far greater than others. It is easy to find ourselves overwhelmed when trying to chase these goals. There is simply so much to do and most of us may not have an idea of what we must do and how to achieve said goals. To make things easier, we use SMART goals to make them more achievable.

SMART stands for:

- Specific
- Measurable
- Achievable
- Relevant
- Time-bound

By setting SMART goals, you allow yourself to plan and set goals that you can then divide into smaller tasks. Not only do you get a systematic layout of what you are supposed to do to achieve said goal, but you also get to experience success each time you complete a milestone.

Take Responsibility

One of the biggest problems we all face is that of taking responsibility. If something goes wrong, we are quick to run away from taking responsibility and find something to blame on for the failure. This kind of mindset will never allow you to go further in life. For any successful leader and entrepreneur, it is a given that they take responsibility for every word and action that comes from them even if the result fetches failure.

There are things that fall within your control and then there are things that fall outside it. Mentally tough people accept both of these for what they are. If it is something that falls within their control, they will take responsibility, but anything that falls outside their control, they will acknowledge it right away. Obviously, there is no point in taking responsibility for the market, economy, weather, or even other people. The only thing you can take responsibility for is you, and that alone is enough.

Stop Overanalyzing

Another problem that I have seen people do over and over again is to overanalyze gain or loss right away. Something goes wrong, "it's my fault" and if something goes right "I did it." Either way, you end up harming yourself.

For anything that goes in your favor, do not boast about it. Instead, let your success speak for you. However, should things go south, stop blaming yourself for the loss or mistake. It is natural for people to fail, however, if you attach the blame to yourself, you are limiting the possibility of finding the actual error. Now, people would cease to identify the problem and focus completely upon you, accepting you as the party to be blamed for the failure. Overanalyzing matters, especially the negative outcomes, will lead you to suffer from depression, anxiety, and stress.

Stop "Needing"

Another problem most of us have is that we fail to realize the difference between wanting something and needing something.

You often come across a situation where you feel like you want to buy yourself something. Then, there are moments where you tell yourself you need something, even if you do not want it. To become mentally strong, stop thinking that you need something in life that is not essential. It is perfectly okay to want something and carry out the necessary actions just so you could go on and acquire it. However, if you feel like you need something in life that is anything besides the basic things a human being needs to survive, you probably don't need it at all.

You may want a car, but if you live in an area where there are accessible transit options, there is no need to buy one. You can always use public transport or settle for Uber or other alternative modes for transportation. You may think you need to buy yourself a house, but millions of people continue to live peacefully and lavishly in apartments as well. It is just a matter of figuring out what you require in life and what may go on to deviate you from your goals.

Seek Help When Required

There is no shame in admitting that you need help with something. Of course, you cannot expect yourself to be skilled at everything nor is it humanly possible for you to handle every single aspect of the business yourself. There will come time where you may need help, whether for personal matters or professional ones. In either case, be sure to seek out help from those who are the right kind of people.

There is no point in seeking out help regarding your finances from someone who has no idea what finance is. Such advice would only go on to serve you with more doubts and questions than answers. Where possible, hire a professional to get the job done properly.

Avoiding Self-Pity

If you allow yourself to be succumbed by self-pity, you will end up in a messy and emotional situation. You will no longer be in a zone where you would be able to take meaningful decisions in life. You will find yourself lost, trapped in a loop. To break out of the loop, stop pitying yourself.

Learn from Your Past

The time that couldn't come back. There is no point in spending any part of your present recalling your past and crying about it. We have all made mistakes, and we have all lost someone we love at some point in time. It is only a natural occurrence. However, there are always lessons that we can certainly take from our past and bring it to our present and future.

Whatever mistakes you may have made, whatever may have gone wrong somewhere in your past, learn from it. Do not be judgmental about your past. Think of it as a phase that came to pass. All you can do about it now is to learn what went wrong, and how such a situation can be avoided or improved upon should it come back in the future.

Your past becomes a part of you and the only purpose it is supposed to serve is to teach you. If you keep on repeating the same mistakes over and over again, you are clearly missing out on learning from your past mistakes. It is also possible that you may not view certain actions or decisions as errors. Discuss with someone who can help you analyze things without bias. Only then will you be able to use the new perspective and figure out your mistakes. Once done, start improving upon them or learn how to avoid them completely.

Emotions Versus Logic

They say that women use emotions to think while men rely on logic alone. I say that is just nonsense. I have seen women far more capable of using logic than most men and I have seen men holding far too many emotions than women, and based on that, I know the notoriously famous claim is baseless.

Whether you are a man or a woman, you have the capacity to hold both emotions and logic. You can base most of your decisions using emotions or logic or a mixture of both. If you ask me, I would opt to stick with a mixture of both.

It is necessary that you remain calm and composed in the face of tragedy, problems and challenges because if you allow your emotions to take over, you will most likely end up making a blunder that you would regret for the rest of your life. This isn't only applicable in a professional setting, but even matters relating to your personal life can easily be sabotaged by your emotions.

To make the best decision possible, keep a check on your emotions and think rationally. If you are unable to do so, meditate a little before moving on. I will talk all about meditation later in the book as that is one of the finest exercises you can use to calm yourself down quickly and regain control of the situation.

Strike a healthy balance between the two because you need both to work your way through many challenges and obstacles along the way. Most will require you to use logic but something will genuinely require you to be in touch with your emotions. Know when you need to use logic and when you need to rely on your emotions.

Improving Your Brain

Apart from the above, there are other things that you can do to further help your brain improve itself. Below are some of the finest ways to get started. Once again, everything that I explain and teach, know that each of these will take time to fully manifest and bring forth the results. As long as you are consistent, you should be able to see the results soon enough.

Exploiting Your Weaknesses

There are some of us who prefer working in the morning and then there are those who prefer to work late in the night. Challenge yourself to tackle some tasks that require you to be creative or use your brain at odd times. For people who work in the morning, set aside a task or two and do these in the evening or night. For the night owls, find something that you should do in the morning.

You might be wondering why I am stating the above. By doing so, you unlock newer possibilities and train your brain to be active even in times where you would otherwise be busy doing something unproductive. It also helps you gain potentially good and surprising results. Care must be taken not to assign yourself any analytical task as that may be counterproductive. Only stick to tasks that require you to use creativity.

Use Memory Games

Our memory continues to deteriorate every single day. This mostly happens because of the wear and tear of cells that comes naturally with age. However, what others fail to realize is that the lesser we train our memory the quicker it will deteriorate. A great way to ensure that doesn't happen is to use good memory games.

These days, you can find many memory games throughout the internet. If you are an android user or someone who fancies iOS, you can find millions of apps that help you boost your memory skills. They are fun, and they are surprisingly productive as well.

The better your memory, the more efficient you will become in life. You will then be able to remember most of the small details if not all and recall those upon will to make decisions based upon those details. This will help you excel at what you do and be an efficient worker or businessperson.

Mnemonics

For those who may not know what mnemonics are, these are essentially memory devices that you use to recall something. They help and aid with memory retention and use elaborative encoding, imagery and retrieval clues.

They help you to further stretch your brain and improve memory retention. This is particularly helpful if you are someone who meets a lot of people every now and then. Some easy ways would be to tie names with professions, such as:

- Sara the supervisor
- Linda the lawyer
- David the doctor

By doing so, you force your brain to work a little harder at first, and then it becomes extremely easy to recall names or professions or any other piece of information that may be crucial.

Raise Eyebrows

You may be a bit surprised, but raising eyebrows is actually a very healthy exercise. Of course, you may not find doing this appropriate in crowded situations, but when you can, do it. This may seem extremely obnoxious at first, but once you start doing this, you will experience a slight adrenaline boost. Consider this as an SOS button that helps you to feel brighter and more alert in seconds.

Read More

Do not waste your time reading something that may not offer anything valuable to you. Find something that helps you become a better person. Read something that encourages you to push your known boundaries and explore newer venues. There is far more that you can achieve in life than what you may think. That unknown is only found when you find the will to explore and push your boundaries further.

New Hobbies

Not everything in life must be serious. Our life is never complete until we include some fun and interesting activities into the mix. That is where our hobbies come into play. You may already have a few hobbies, but it never hurts to find and explore new ones.

If you always wanted to learn how to play guitars, now would be a good time to get started. If you wanted to learn how to crochet and create some incredible crafts at home, get started. There is no better time than now to do just that.

You may be wondering how on earth engaging in new hobbies helps one to become mentally strong. By exploring something new and learning it, it opens a new territory within your brain, allowing it to evolve and grow stronger. By feeding it with new and interesting information, your mind is forced to retain this information and use more of its capacity, eventually increasing your overall knowledge, retention power, and skills.

Eat Healthy

I cannot stress upon this point enough. There is no other way to say this, but if you do not eat healthy, your mind will start to suffer, ultimately losing most of its functions.

Eat food that helps you to boost your memory and brain functions. I would always recommend that you stick to a balanced diet and get the nutrients you need that boost your bodily systems. However, consult a doctor in case you are someone who suffers from allergies or underlying ailments.

Exercise

Physical and mental exercises are must for a healthy lifestyle. Not only do these allow you to feel good, look good, and be more active, but they also help you feel ready and eager. You will find yourself working at your optimum level the more you exercise.

It must be noted that exercises are meant to be done every day. You need to commit to the idea that you will exercise daily and remain consistent. Break the consistency and you will soon find yourself back to square one.

It is through exercise that our body's blood circulation improves and flows more smoothly. This helps in ensuring that our organs and body parts get their fresh supply of blood regularly, allowing us to feel active and healthy.

Sleep Well

There are many who may continue to cut on their sleep, just to make sure that they can get up early in the morning. If getting up early is so important, it is best to sleep early. You can compromise on a lot of things, sleep isn't one of them.

According to statistics by the American Sleep Association (ASA), 50 to 70 million US adults suffer from sleep disorder (American Sleep Association, n.d.). That is an alarming number of people suffering from sleep disorder.

Not sleeping well, or having an irregular sleep pattern causes you to suffer from issues like insomnia, drowsiness and many other ailments. It is also worth noticing that your brain is affected negatively if you cut down on your sleep hours.

Adults generally required between seven to nine hours sleep a day. Anything less than that is neither healthy nor recommended. Of course, the same is true for anything above that range as that too can indicate something wrong with your sleep pattern. In order to be mentally strong, you need to allow your mind to gain the rest it needs to rejuvenate and regain its strength to function the next day.

By working on all of the above, you will see a significant improvement within yourself and your mental toughness levels. You will start viewing the world more positively, more actively and will be able to better manage your emotions, time and energy. Take it from someone who has gone through extreme situations and scenarios, and has regained rhythm after doing all of the above to become more mentally tough.

Each of the above components that I have mentioned, I continue to use them regularly. These have helped me gain mental toughness, and, as a result, they have helped me to be more successful in my life. Yes, the struggle was time consuming, and some of the activities really seemed like I was wasting my time shooting in the dark. However, with patience and consistency, the results started to emerge. With one success after the other, my life changed right before my eyes, and just in a year, I felt like a completely new person. I was no longer the kind of person who would easily get distracted or suppressed or confused. Now, I handled my emotions better, made better decisions, and above all, started to lead a healthier life. I found a new purpose, one that actually made sense to me, and I picked up a few good hobbies along the way that help me feel good about myself and provide a much-needed break when I need one.

The path to success is one that one must explore on their own. I can draw you a map but it is you who must walk the path and do all that is needed to ensure you see matters through. In this chapter, I gave you a taste of how you can change a weaker mind and convert it into one that is mentally tough. In the next chapter, I will walk you through some of the most common traps people fall for when trying to pursue mental toughness. It is imperative that you identify these and learn what you should be beware of.

Chapter 3:

Common Traps for Mental toughness

It is easy to find yourself lost in the world of mental toughness. This pursuit often leads you to find materials, concepts, and ideas that may actually be counterproductive, experimental in nature, or based on rumours. At times, it gets really hard to figure out whether what you read is authentic or otherwise. Fortunately, I have already gone through these experiences, and my research into mental toughness has allowed me to be in a position where I can guide you and anyone who wishes to learn what you must do and what you must avoid at all cost.

While the remainder of the chapters are based on what you should do, this chapter is specifically dedicated to learning some of the most common traps that exist for mental toughness. In this chapter, you will learn:

- Things you must always be aware of and avoid
- Ways to go about mental toughness

- Identifying things that cause problems

With that said, let us start and look into each one of these.

The Traps to Avoid

If you feel like you have been bombarded with knowledge and that it is becoming a bit cumbersome to keep pace, it is perfectly okay to take a break. A lot of people continue to read on, not because they are trying to gain knowledge, but because they just wish to get it over with so that they never have to touch the book ever again. If that was your intention, you will eventually get the job done, but what good would that do to you if you're not consistently reinforcing those skills?

Mental toughness isn't just about persevering in the face of difficulty and keep on going, but it is to gain the most out of the situation and use positivity to keep the momentum going. Of course, every human being has a set limit that is impossible to breach. According to the BBC, studies suggest that an average person can only concentrate for as long as ninety minutes before they need a fifteen minute break (Williams, 2017).

The above is a fact that most of us, intentionally or otherwise, tend to overlook. Our brain can only process so much information in a single stretch. It, just like our body, needs a break. There are many stories, articles, and even some books that go on to claim that you should push your boundaries and keep on working. While that may be true and actually a good idea, do not overlook the need to take a break.

By taking a quick fifteen minute break, you allow your brain to process all the information it has gained. It is just like filling an empty cup with water. If you continue to pour more, it will eventually start spilling out. In order to make room for more water, you must first empty the cup and then continue the process. Similarly, once your mind gets its break, it stores the information and regains the energy and capacity to accept more knowledge coming its way, without compromising any of the previously acquired knowledge.

Born Tough

There is yet another rumour that continues to reside in many places, especially on the internet. This rumor is based on an idea that people are born with mental toughness, and those who lack do so because they cannot develop mental toughness on their own. Once again, this is nothing more than a rumour.

Researchers around the world have come to a unanimous conclusion that mental toughness isn't inherited, and that it can be gained, developed and mastered by anyone who is willing to do what is required. In 2011, a renowned paper in the *Journal of Sports Psychology in Action* went on to confirm that anyone can develop mental toughness, as long as a challenging and a supportive environment is created that goes on to promote personal responsibility, self-reflection, and problem-solving skills (Sutton, 2019).

Mental toughness is generally something that athletes excel at. They face some of the toughest contestants from around the world, but they neither allow themselves to feel unnerved or overwhelmed in the presence of others. They continue to tell themselves that they have trained for such a position and that they have what it takes to go out there and conquer the stage. Naturally, such a confidence and positive mindset boosts their morale and helps them make rational and logical decisions. Once again, they do not worry about the results. Win or not, they still get the job done. This is why you might see athletes sprinting for the finish line even if they are the last ones running. They do not give in and give it their absolute best because that's what they train themselves for.

It is perfectly okay if your best isn't better than the others, you were never in to win every time. With every failure, you get a chance to reflect upon your weaknesses and work on them. Each one of us is unique in our own respective ways. All you need to do is to find what makes you unique, what your strengths are, and how you can improve on your weaknesses.

Procrastination Kills

There is no denying the fact that procrastination is one of the most common evils in existence today. Everyone does it, everyone knows about it, and everyone wants to get rid of it.

Procrastinating on things is never, and I repeat, never a good thing. Procrastination can only bring you harm or invite more trouble. Whether you are trying to skip doing something that has been asked of you or you are trying to delay something because you think you have something else that takes priority, procrastination simply shows how weak of a willpower you have. Let me give you an example to further highlight what I am on about.

You spent the previous night drinking with your mates at your favorite bar. You got home, and you barely remember how you got into bed. All you know is that your alarm starts to ring at 5:30 AM in the morning. You wake up and find you have a pounding headache and mild grogginess. What do you think you will do? Will you hit the snooze button for another thirty to sixty minutes or will you turn the alarm off and actually get out of bed to go out and exercise? Despite almost everyone claiming to do the former, only 20% of the readers would actually go out and exercise. The rest would hit the snooze button and go back to sleep, thinking it's okay to miss a day at the gym.

You miss a day today, and a few days later, you will miss another day. Now, you have missed out two days. These two will become three in the following week and the numbers will keep climbing until you no longer go to the gym. Why? You decided it is okay to procrastinate a little just to get in some extra sleep. If you had the willpower to tolerate pain and had the will to take responsibility for your actions, you may have actually continued to exercise and workout in a gym.

In order to gain mental toughness, know that procrastination cannot be allowed into your life. Procrastination is indirectly proportional to mental toughness where one rises and the other falls. From this point on, you get to decide which of the two would you rather have in life.

It Takes Time

Earlier in the book, I talked about how to break goals into smaller, more achievable tasks. Athletes normally use this approach to start working towards something big. Let's assume that an athlete starts training for a 100 mile run. It is humanly impossible to wake up one day and decide you will do the run that given day or even within the same week if you have never run more than a mile in a go.

Everything in life takes time. There is no point in rushing towards your goal. A lot of people are far too eager that they try and jump ahead of their own plans just so they can reach their goals faster. This can often fetch negative results and these would be the kind of results that you may not have planned for. If you are not mentally tough enough, you may find yourself facing a lot of problems, sometimes a bit more than you can handle. Do not fall for such a trap. Take things slowly and follow a concrete plan of action.

Get Started

I was the kind of person who would put together some of the finest plans in life. However, I would plan and then sit around, procrastinate and wait for the right time that never really came. It wasn't that I didn't want to start working on my plan, but it was fear of failing that held me back from taking my first step.

Use my experience to learn that in order to move forward, you must first move. It does not matter if your first step is in the opposite direction. Unless you find the courage to take that first step, you will never know which direction is the one you need to follow and which one is it that you need to avoid. Do not wait for opportune moments because time is a luxury none of us can afford to lose. You can put together all the money in the world, but you will still not be able to buy a second of time for yourself.

If you believe you are on to something, or you believe that you have a solid plan laid out, start acting on it right away and move forward with positivity and an open mind. Let the challenges come because no matter what you face, you will see through those problems and achieve your goals. No one said things will get easier, and I am not here to tell you otherwise either.

Mental Toughness Versus Stubbornness

There is a fine line that divides mental toughness and stubbornness. Unfortunately, a lot of people still end up blurring that line and finding themselves on the wrong side. These two traits are completely different and have little to no relation to each other.

We already know what mental toughness is, and that's why I will not waste your time telling you the same thing all over again. Stubbornness, on the other hand, is something different. It is a mental state where a person refuses to cave in, back down out of an argument, and is willing to do anything and everything to prove his point. Those who are stubborn often lead very complicated lives. They suffer in personal and professional aspects of life. They make some of the worst decisions that often lead them to run right into trouble.

You may have heard about a company named Nokia. It was once the king of the hill. No other company on earth could match the might and innovation of the company. Their products were incredible to use, extremely sophisticated for their time, and everyone wanted a Nokia phone. Then, as fate would have it, things changed. The world started exploring android and iOS platforms and companies that were once dwelling in the shadows started to emerge into the spotlight. Nokia, on the other hand, remained stubborn. They refused to change their operating system and refused to follow a new direction other companies were taking. What happened next was something beyond anyone's expectation. Nokia, within a matter of a couple of years, was brought down on its knees as it raised the white flag and accepted defeat. Samsung, Apple, Huawei and other smartphone makers dominated the world while the former king of the hill was pushed back into the pages of history. The company management refused to acknowledge their errors and refused to adapt to the change. Their stubbornness brought down a multi-billion dollar empire hard.

Learning from this fact, know that stubbornness is not always appreciated or rewarded. Times change and so should we. To be mentally tough, stubbornness needs to be side-lined because it can get in the way of rational thinking. It is because of our emotions that we normally become stubborn, and as we learned earlier, we are to maintain a healthy balance between the two. Do not allow your emotions to control you. Do that and you automatically wipe away stubbornness from life.

Barring Laziness

By now, you should have a fair idea of just how terrible a disease laziness can be. It would be a good time to share with you just how laziness almost ended ruining my life for good.

I already confessed that I wasn't born with mental toughness. I had my evils to worry about and every goal I set would eventually fail. This paved way for procrastination and laziness, the kind of which can literally bring anyone's life to a complete halt. People would tell me that I am wasting my time away and not taking things seriously. I did take everything that was happening seriously, but I wasn't doing much about it.

The fact of the matter is that I would sleep more than needed, find it extremely hard to get out of bed, eat at my own chosen time, and would always find it cumbersome to even do the most simplest of tasks. I was the perfect example of what laziness looks like in real life.

Every single day, someone would pop in and criticize me for my non-serious attitude towards life. This was okay at first as I would not at all be bothered about what others said. I would always tell myself "they don't know what I am doing" and things like "I'll show them one day and silence them." While there was some motivation to be vindicated, there was no actual action that I was taking to do that.

I had brilliant ideas, but my laziness ensured that I never could pursue them. I wasn't even scared of taking those first few steps, but it was my laziness that held me back. To me, the only thing that mattered was my comfort zone. Whether I cared enough to admit it or not, I'd let anything that would fall outside my comfort zone pass.

My laziness knew no bounds. I would unwillingly end up ignoring and avoiding virtually every single thing that required me to get out of my room. There I was thinking that I was preparing myself for something greater, but little did I know that I was being held captive by my laziness.

For any successful person, laziness is a downright killer. You can either allow success to be a part of your life or you can choose to be lazy, procrastinate, and let things slip right through your fingers. Had I not changed my life the way I did, I might have still remained in that room, without a job, without a career, and without anything good in life.

One of the biggest problems we face today is that of accepting that there is life outside the bubble we create for ourselves. If we truly wish to conquer challenges, grab all possible opportunities and prepare ourselves for success, we must learn to step outside our comfort zones and explore the world. The two cannot be found in the same place. Once again, it is a decision that you must make on your own. If you wish to be successful, say goodbye to your comfort zone and laziness for good. To help you out, here are some incredible tips and methods to eliminate laziness from life:

- Wake up early
- Exercise in the early hours of the morning
- Eat healthy
- Meditate
- Socialize

These are some of the most common things to do, but the results are always beyond fascinating. You do not have to take my word for it, try it yourself. You'd be surprised at just how much you are missing out on life.

In the next chapter, we will talk about one of the most crucial aspects of mental toughness. It is what pushes us to take actions and convert our visions, dreams and ideas into a living breathing reality. It isn't magic, but it is something as good as.

Chapter 4:

Mental Toughness and Willpower

So far, we learned a lot about mental toughness. We learned what defines someone as mentally tough and what it takes to gain mental toughness. We then moved on to learn about what a weak mind is and how one can go about addressing the issue. Later, we learned about some of the most common misunderstandings, rumours and traps that a lot of people end up falling for, and we learned how to avoid these. Now, it is time to address what may arguably be the most important component - willpower.

Understanding Willpower

Willpower is defined as the ability that helps you to resist short-term temptations to ensure that you meet your long-term goals. It is one of the most powerful abilities within every human being, but despite that, there are countless number of people who never realize the true extent of power willpower has to offer. Some go spending their whole lifetimes trying to look for things that could help them become a better person, and they do not realize that they never needed to search anywhere else. They all had willpower within them, waiting for it to be used and benefited from.

Willpower is what drives your vehicle of life from here to wherever there is. It is through willpower that you find the courage and energy to do things that would otherwise seem impossible to do.

Willpower is what overrides your desires, wants, and needs. It is what helps you choose to do something you believe is more important as opposed to something that tempts you. It isn't necessarily limited to smoking or drinking or other leisurely activities either. Willpower is what great leaders and success stories continue to use and thrive with every single day. It is willpower that helps you make some of life's toughest decisions, and helps you become mentally tougher with each passing day.

Let us imagine an athlete who is running long distances and is preparing for a major event that can very well change his life for good. Athletes may very well be trained to gain mental toughness, however, their willpower is what sees them run for the last gruelling mile. It is their willpower that pushes them to go beyond their known threshold of pain, find that extra burst of energy and motivation to cross the line and make history. Take the willpower away and they will immediately give in to the pain that develops after running for such a long distance. By using willpower, the athlete did not give into the desire of calling it a day and stopping. His body chose to push on and make it to the end.

Pain is essentially our body's response to some changes that may not sit well with the mind. Whether you are stretching your muscles, running far too long and fast, or even lifting weights, you are exerting some force on your body. To adjust and accept this force, our muscles move and provide us with the strength needed to endure the force. The longer we demand our muscles to provide us strength, the more they start to stretch and strain. Eventually, our mind starts interpreting this disturbance as pain. Many other things start feeding our mind with information, and almost all of this information forces the brain to make a decision to either continue doing whatever we were doing (willpower) or stop. If we have willpower, we will continue with the exercise for a while longer before ultimately stopping. While the additional exercise may not seem like much, especially as these additional efforts last a few minutes at most, they actually help you do more than what your body thinks is possible.

"The last three or four reps is what makes the muscle grow. This area of pain divides the champion from someone else who is not a champion. That's what most people lack, having the guts to go on and just say they'll go through the pain no matter what happens."
- Arnold Schwarzenegger

Mental toughness and willpower are interlinked with one another. While one creates a persona, the other keeps it going. Where one finds ways to get the job done, the other ensures the required actions are taken. If you feel like you lack willpower, don't worry. I am about to teach you how to develop your willpower through some incredibly easy tips and suggestions. Once again, consistency is the key to ensure results. Do not complain if you are unable to maintain consistency and not find results.

Building Willpower

Contrary to popular belief, you can actually increase your willpower. As always, consistency is the key. You cannot expect to see the results coming your way within a day or two of practicing.

To bring any kind of change in your life, you need willpower. Whether it is to shed weight, start a business, make relative decisions, or anything relatively important, you need willpower to get started.

One of the biggest reasons we lose willpower happens to be bad habits. You may have the finest lifestyle in the world, but you will always be lacking the willpower to take matters in hand and make decisions that go on to benefit you. As long as these exist, you cannot go on to achieve anything great in life.

Let us consider willpower as a muscle. It is a muscle that we go on to use and change our habits with, thus changing or eliminating habits that give us bad outcomes. Our bad habits are generally controlled by our subconscious mind. Anything that is controlled by this part of the brain, it happens automatically, even if you are not aware you are doing it. Remember the car driving example I used earlier on in the book? Our bad habits happen in exactly the same fashion.

This is where willpower steps in and breaks away these habits. By doing so, it helps us replace these with better, more productive habits that can actually bring us some benefits. Of course, this is a bit of an issue for those who may lack willpower, however, here are some great ways through which you can increase your willpower and start breaking away the negative habits within you.

Reinforce Benefits of Achieving Your Goals

What I am essentially asking you to do here is to create a habit within yourself that constantly, and I do mean constantly, reminds you of the benefits of achieving your set goals.

Remind yourself every now and then the reasons why you wish to achieve said goals and how doing so would go on to change your lifestyle in the future. Through this exercise, you strengthen your desire to pursue these goals, and that makes it a lot easier to resist all kinds of temptations that you may find yourself with.

You can find tons of ways to set reminders. I personally use fridge magnets and stick little post-it notes that I look upon every time I walk past the fridge. If you prefer to use your inner voice as a reminder, you can do the same as well. However, for those who may be considering using their inner voice, it is easy to get distracted long enough to actually miss out a much-needed motivation. Keep something with yourself that reminds your inner voice to do its job. You can attach some importance to a ring, a sticker on your cell phone, a piece of thread or a keyring, whatever works for you.

Whatever method you use, the principle remains the same. You must constantly and continuously remind yourself of the benefits you will go on to experience and enjoy once you achieve your goals. It may sound a little too repetitive, but at times, we must reinforce concepts to our brain, feed it again and again until it starts familiarizing itself with the information and starts accepting that. Besides, we are not trying to push our conscious mind to do the work. We are actually trying to engage our subconsciousness into the mix because once your subconsciousness is involved, things get a lot easier. I can write a complete book on how the subconscious belief system works and how a simple intention can often go on to do wonders, but I may do that later on. For now, know that you must feed information to your subconsciousness over and over again until it is engaged. How would you know if it is engaged, I hear you ask? I assure you, the day you start feeling surprised at how easy things are turning out to be, know that your subconscious is at work.

Through repetition, you develop a greater willpower to start moving forward and achieve your goals in time.

Willpower + Self-Control - They're Incremental

If you go on to start working on your willpower and increase it in a specific area, it will automatically start producing better results in other areas as well. You may be working to improve your willpower to make better decisions, especially ones that are generally hard to make on your own. However, by doing so, you will also witness a rise in your willpower in other regions such as asking questions, voicing out opinions, or raising your hand first to contribute something to the meeting, even if it sounds simple.

The reason I highlighted that is simple is that there are far too many scenarios in life where you may face a multitude of problems. You may often be caught in such a situation where you will have no idea where to start from. The good news is that by developing your willpower, you will also gain self-control. Having self-control means that you will be able to direct your attention and refine your focus on a specific aspect, allowing you to make better decisions and dealing with the problems one by one. The good news doesn't stop there either. Once you solve a problem, your willpower will gain intensity, and that would automatically make solving the next problem a little easier. The cycle will continue until you have solved all your problems, and before you know it, you'll be wondering why on earth were you nervous in the first place.

Nourishment is Vital

I have spoken about this earlier on in the book. In order to be healthy, physically and mentally, you need to start eating healthy. The concept of a balanced diet is one that allows you to consume all vital nutrients that your body, including your mind, needs to improve function and carry on. The more they are deprived of these nutrients, the worse they perform. This is why you will see successful people hitting the gym bright and early in the morning, eating all kinds of fruits, vegetables, nuts and energy bars while consuming natural juices. This isn't just a lifestyle that they choose for themselves, it is far more than that.

Have you ever wondered why some of the most successful people in the world continue to make decisions after decisions that astonish and surprise the world over and over again? It is because they choose a lifestyle that ensures their body, especially the mind, gets all the nutrients it needs to operate at optimum levels.

Nourishment is one of the most effective ways to increase willpower as well. How does that work? The science is rather simple. If your blood-sugar level drops, which it does when you are hungry, your min and other vital organs take a toll. They stop functioning at their optimum levels. They are no longer working at full capacity partially because of the low blood-sugar levels but mostly because they are no longer able to draw the kind of energy they need to get the work done as they normally would. You will, therefore, experience lack of concentration, reduced self-control and at times weakness. To ensure that you always have the right kind of willpower for the job, make it a point in life that you will eat adequately. This would allow you to have adequate blood-sugar levels, assisting you in doing all that is important at an optimum level.

Positive Mindset

Without a positive mindset, you cannot expect your willpower to work for you at all. A lot of people often confuse mental toughness with a positive mindset. They may be interlinked, but they are not one and the same thing.

Having a positive mindset and maintaining it helps you build on your willpower. It allows you to see the brighter side of things, hence increasing motivation and driving your willpower through the roof. You might ask why you need a positive mindset if you have the willpower to carry out tasks.

Even with enormous willpower, you may often end up making mistakes because, let's all face it, you are just a human being. We are bound to make mistakes every now and then. Now, if you do end up making a mistake that costs you something in return, a positive mindset will help you negotiate such a situation with positivity and extract some valuable lesson from the experience to make your future more secure. However, take away the positive mindset and you will start beating yourself up for a mistake that may or may not be yours to begin with. You will spend a significant amount of time blaming yourself and your lack of something that caused you to suffer a loss. That is counterproductive and will lead you into all kinds of problems such as:

- Anxiety
- Depression
- Stress
- Confusion
- Feeling belittled or embarrassed

You always need a positive mindset to handle such situations both logically and productively. You may be a person who feels you have a lot of emotions riding on something, but using a positive mindset, you will ensure that you do not cloud your judgement and make logical rational decisions and move on.

Motivate Yourself

There are millions of ways you can motivate yourself. One of the most popular tools to do so is the Risk-Reward tool. The idea is that you set yourself with goals that have both risks and rewards. If you fail at the task, you will need to do what the potential risk was set initially, regardless of how bad or embarrassing it may be. However, if you go on to fulfill the goal and achieve said targets, you will set a reward for yourself. Whatever the reward may be, you must ensure you take it. There is no need to be generous and let it slide because that goes against the idea of the tool.

To give you an example, I hate cleaning bathrooms. I loathe the idea of scrubbing away on the toilet seat, clearing out the clutter and cleaning every inch of the tile that clearly isn't the most hygienic one on the planet. Let's assume that I want to lose weight, about ten pounds in the next five months. If I am able to reduce my weight by ten pounds by the end of the stipulated time, I will go on a week-long vacation as my reward. However, if I lose, I will scrub every toilet, every bathroom in the house. Now, this goal will have some meaning for me. This risk-reward tool will ensure that I am always on my toes, ready to get the task done. Whether I am doing my tasks because I fear what I would have to do if I fail or because I am genuinely interested in the reward, I am motivated to ensure I do not fail.

Motivation plays a very critical role in life. It is also a great tool to increase your willpower. Above is just one of many ways through which you can help yourself get the job done and gain the willpower you need to see matters through.

Naturally, there are times where you may feel well short of motivation. You may often find it hard to locate reasons that could help you motivate yourself. When you find such moments in life, here are a few things that you can recall and draw some motivation from:

- You live in a time that has the most available resources and opportunities

- If you worry about a job, you can always create your own job that you are truly passionate about
- You can choose to have a healthy lifestyle any given day
- You have the ability to foster and develop positive relationships
- You have a lot to be thankful for such as a roof, food, water, clothes, et cetera
- You have the power to make a difference in someone's life

There is so much in life to be motivated from. Regardless of what your financial standings may be, despite what ailments some of you may have, if you are able to read this line, know that you are already doing far better than a lot of people across the globe. There are those who cannot even afford to eat heartily even once in a day. There are those who cannot afford to live inside a four-walled structure. Think about it - we are blessed to have so many luxuries already.

With that said, it is time for us to move on to our next chapter. This chapter spoke all about how to develop willpower and how it goes on to benefit us. We learned all that we can do to help us develop and strengthen our willpower as well as some tips and tricks that can work in collaboration to produce some truly spectacular results. Now that you have learned all the fundamentals, it is time to start learning how to become mentally tough. The next chapter will dive into all the important aspects and teach you what you can do to become mentally tougher.

Chapter 5

How to Build Mental Toughness and Why

So far, you have learned all you need to know before you can get started with learning how to build mental toughness. I will not beat around the bush nor drag things unnecessarily just to ensure that we get straight to the point and get started. I could have done this in the first chapter, but had I done that, you would have missed out on some key elements and components, all of which chip in to the entire mental toughness concept. Now that you know the fundamentals, learning how to build mental toughness will be a lot easier. With that said, let's get started right away!

Building Mental Toughness

Everyone in existence has a certain degree of mental toughness that they use every day. It varies from one person to another. You may feel like you are in control of everything when you are within your comfort zone but as soon as you step outside your comfort zone, you feel like you are no longer in control of anything. This is a common problem that most of us face.

My research led me through some of the most astonishing and surprising facts that I never knew I had. We have already discussed most of them earlier in the book, but there is plenty more where that came from.

Building on mental toughness is important, and I am not saying that just to retain your attention either. I may not know who you are, but I can still guarantee that you, or anyone else for that matter, need mental toughness within your life, professional or personal. There are far too many things that happen every single day, from work-related matters to personal development, that we need to be in complete control of and manage. To face these challenges and changes, we need mental toughness.

If achieving success was so easy, no one would be complaining about how they feel unsuccessful or how they are unable to chase their dreams. Most give up the pursuit right in the start because they develop a false sense of failure. They believe that they are destined to fail and that's where things start going wrong. Failure is a part of life and I can quote millions of such examples and success stories that have emerged out of the ashes. They did so not because they had financial support or guidance, but because they refused to give into the idea that they had met their match. They refused to give up.

Consistency, momentum and mental toughness is what saw them make breakthroughs after breakthroughs. If they were able to do that, so can we.

There are quite a few things that stand between us and our ability to build on mental toughness. One of the key elements is that of self-belief.

Self-Limiting Beliefs

By the age of eight, an average person develops around 90% of the subconscious belief system that directly influences the decisions we make as adults. This means that over 90% of the decisions we make as adults, professionals, parents and partners, we are never really in control of these. Our subconscious belief system makes us feel like it is the right thing to do even though it may not be. This also highlights a problem, and that is the lack of willpower and mental toughness. We are quickly drawn to follow something that is familiar as opposed to exploring something that may be unknown and new. This is exactly why we often drive through longer routes, not because they may have lesser traffic or that they are more scenic, but because we are quite familiar with how that road is going to be.

This is, in a way, a system that limits us and our sense of exploration. For anyone to be mentally tough, we need to let go of any belief that limits us. To put it in easier words, if you think you cannot do something, stop thinking and let that thought go. Find the courage and will to pursue this new idea. What you may believe to be hard or difficult might actually turn out to be just the thing you needed all this time to get your first breakthrough.

If you do not change things, change will force you to change your ways, and that is not the kind of situation you want to be in. By limiting your ability to think and act, you are barring many opportunities to come your way. Instead of beating yourself up for something that you were led to believe could not be done, try and take a step forward. Reaffirm yourself that you have what it takes to do this. Let yourself know that this is just another challenge that you will face gladly and learn from. You do not have to be the smartest guy in the room to become successful. In fact, a lot of successful people hire smarter people to do the hard work for them. However, in order to do that, you first need to prove to yourself and your mind that you have the mental toughness to break out of your perceived limitations and explore newer avenues.

To give you yet another example, the idea of writing a book was completely insane. I once questioned the idea of how I would be able to write a book. I thought that I did not have what it takes to get the job done, but my mental toughness and willpower, they helped me to take a step forward. I started slowly and created an outline. Then, I started with the introduction, and before you know it, I created a momentum. That momentum then pushed me forward, kept me going, and it has done well so far.

Your self-limiting thoughts, of which there would be many, are only there to limit you. These serve you with no actual advantage and must be replaced with positivity. Here is a little challenge for you to work on:

Take an hour of your time and write down all such self-limiting ideas and theories you may have. Take a note of all ideas that you think you cannot do because you perceive you aren't smart enough or strong enough to get it done. For the next thirty days, try and do something new every single day using this list. By the end of the thirtieth day, you will come out with a fresh new perspective. You will end the month knowing that you explored newer avenues. Who knows, you might just stumble across something that genuinely provides you with opportunities worth exploring in the future.

All or Nothing

It is only natural that we, out of frustration, often allow the all or nothing mindset to come into play. We often feel like we have been doing something for far too long with little to no results at all. To break out of the chain, we let our emotions get the better of us and push us into making decisions where we put everything on the line. It could end with us winning back more than what we have or losing everything. Either way, it isn't a good idea.

The latter part, where one would end up losing everything, makes sense. No one wants to be in a situation where they have to let go of everything as a result of a terrible decision. However, if you were to win everything back and more in such a short span of time, you will be tempted to do the same over again and increase your gains. It's just like a game of cards at a casino where you may have luckily won the first round. Just because you did so does not mean you will go on to win every other round. There is a greater probability that the next time you go all in, you may actually walk out empty handed. This greed of making more in such a short span of time neither uses any true skill nor comes without risks. One false move and you practically say goodbye to your finances, reputation and fortune.

All or nothing is a negative response, a negative reaction of a situation that you may not be fond of. Do not allow yourself to fall for this trap as this could cause you dearly. It also eats away on willpower and mental toughness as well. Do not let emotions and temptations of winning quick money get the better of you.

Let me put this in another way using a weight loss example. Imagine that I am trying to lose ten pounds of weight in a specific period of time. By the end of this specific period, I manage to lose eight pounds only, and I end the time two pounds short of the target. An all or nothing mindset would practically make me a failure. However, have I truly failed? No, I have not. Even though I was not able to accomplish my goal, I was still able to put in the efforts and shed a significant weight during the same time. I was consistent and passionate about what I was doing.

A mentally tough person will use this as an achievement. They will reassure themselves that they gave their best shot and that they ended up losing a lot of weight and walked away learning something important and valuable.

Failing after you have given your 100% isn't actually failure. People often feel let down but I believe that there is always a brighter side to things. Had I not tried to change my life, I would have actually become a failure, and that's the kind of failure that teaches you nothing. There is no learning curve involved if you are not ready to make a move, take action and commit to something. The all or nothing mindset is something that often pushes us not to take any risk because we are either too frightened by the prospect of losing that we never really pay attention to what we can possibly gain, or we consider ourselves as unworthy and let the opportunity slide. If you really wish to build on your mental toughness, never allow this mindset to be a part of your life. If you are involved in activities where risks come and go, take calculated risks and gauge your success. Even if you fail, you will only lose a fraction of your finances or resources, but in return, you'd gain a lot more knowledge.

Dwelling on the Negative Outcomes

As I mentioned many times, failure is a part of life, and a vital one too. However, if you spend your time dwelling on the past, you are only wasting your own time and energy. You can use the same time and energy to create something more meaningful out of that failure.

Dwelling on negative outcomes not only limits your mental capacity, but it also diminishes it. It has a massive impact on your mental health, and can very well push you into anxiety, stress and depression, just to name a few of the problems will follow. To be mentally tough, you must learn how to ditch your problems in the past and bury them for good.

There is no point in wasting your time on what could've been. There is no way you can reverse time, but what you can do is to move forward from that point on. Dwelling too much on such encounters may often push us to raise the white flag and quit altogether, not the kind of an outcome a leader or an entrepreneur would like to experience.

It is okay if you feel depressed that things did not turn out the way you wanted. It is also okay if you take a bit of a break, but this should never mean that you will give up hopes. Look at Sir James Dyson. He could have given up his chase but he continued to create over 5,000 more failures before he struck gold. Mental toughness allows you to develop perseverance and resilience. Using these would help you stick to the target and the ultimate goal. Furthermore, by planning your way through, you get a decent idea of what takes priority and what you must do to finish a task. Where you find yourself stuck, seek assistance, if possible. You may very well be looking at things from a specific perspective. Let someone shed some light and give you a new perspective to use and learn from. As long as you have the will to learn, you will always find a solution to the problem and move ahead.

Some good ideas to use when you find yourself dwelling too much on past mistakes or results are:

- Speaking to your mentor about the problem and seeking advice
- Gain new perspective
- Limit your dwelling to an hour or a couple at most
- Reassure yourself that you can and will move on, and that this is a phase that will eventually pass
- Distract yourself with something that helps you clear out your mind and empty your emotions

All of these will help you rebuild your focus and build a better mental toughness in the process as well.

Connecting with Your Purpose

Whatever goals you may have set, whatever purpose you believe you have in this world, connect with it. Just because you have set a goal to do something does not mean that you can forget about it or not make the efforts to connect with it. There should be a solid why that you must know and follow. There should be a fairly good reason why you intend to pursue the goals you have set.

As long as there is an intention and a reason why you chase your goals, you will easily be able to focus on them. If you set out massive goals and have no clear explanation as to why you seek them, you will find that you will be easily distracted by other things, and you might just give up the chase right in the middle of the process. All those hours and efforts, therefore, will go in vain.

Whatever your "why" is, it is your inspiration, purpose and motivation that helps you to move towards your goal, work for it and eventually go on to achieve it. Always find out why you want to achieve the goal. If it helps, write these down and let them serve you as reminders. Remember, the more you feed your subconsciousness, the more engaged it will be.

You Are Not Alone

Allow yourself to know that you are not alone in whatever you may be pursuing. Think about the success stories. Oprah Winfrey, perhaps the most famous name in existence, did not build her empire on her own. Bill Gates or Steve Jobs weren't alone either. They had those who shared the ideas and visions.

Whatever goal you may have set for yourself, there are always those who share the same view and take inspiration from your goals. Allow yourself to use this as a reason to unite with these people. You can work alongside them or have them work for you. Together, you will be able to achieve said goals faster and more efficiently than you can as an individual. There is only so much that you, as an individual, can do. There is no shame in finding help and getting some of the difficult tasks done for you instead.

Find Your Mentor

One of the most obvious reasons why people fail despite having great goals and willpower is the lack of mentorship. A mentor is essentially someone who can use their experiences and knowledge and guide you through your journey. Whether you are trying to become the next big real-estate firm or come up with a revolutionary business idea that can very well inspire and move the world, you need a mentor to guide you through.

There was a time when mentors were hard to find, however, you can use great social platforms to seek such inspiring mentors out and approach them. You can get in touch with them and seek out guidance.

At this point, I want to clarify something that many might be wondering. You cannot expect your family members or friends to always be your mentors. There are good reasons for that.

To begin with, someone who holds a heavy enough bias might encourage you in unproductive ways to do something, even if they know it isn't going to work. They do not do that to make you a failure, but they do so because they feel that telling you otherwise may hurt your feelings. This means that their suggestions and guidance is already biased.

Secondly, if friends and family members don't have experience in your chosen field, they may have misconceptions about how that field operates. Of course, if you have someone who has phenomenally successful, that's a massive bonus, but that is rare to find. Never seek guidance from someone who has never gathered the experience and success from the field of your choice. Their recommendations and guidance will only get you stuck in situations you may not have prepared yourself for. Instead, seek out success stories that can provide you with neutral opinions and tell you what is right and what isn't. Your mentor can help you skip through some of the early phases by providing you with all the information you need to get started. Once you are halfway through your goal, you too can start mentoring others and help them move forward just as you were helped by someone else. That is how the cycle works, and it greatly helps many around the world to come closer to success than ever before.

Be Accountable

Whatever actions you take, you must hold yourself accountable. A lot of people think that by being the owner of a firm, they are exempted from explaining to anyone why they chose to do what they did. This often creates more problems than it can solve.

When you take an action, and you know you will be asked questions regarding your decision, you will start looking at the problem or solution from all angles before giving it a go ahead. This will help you analyze your strategies and goals better, allowing you to gauge the pros and cons and find out which outweighs the other. This will also help you make better more confident decisions in life.

Rising Back Up

Setbacks happen, and not just to you and me either. Many major corporations and organizations around the world have experienced their fair share of setbacks. However, those who have mental toughness do not give up. Instead, they ask themselves a few questions that help them to check in on their own mind. These questions are:

- Am I being too hard on myself?
- Is this goal still important to me?
- Are my negative thoughts distorting the view?
- What made this goal important? What was my purpose behind pursuing this goal?
- What positive came out of this setback? (Bollinger, 2020)

With each setback that comes your way, ask yourself some hard questions. Answer as truthfully and honestly as you can as this will allow you to clear things up and help you to move on easily. Setbacks are inevitable and everyone faces them. This means that you aren't the only one who experiences setbacks. To be mentally tough, you must always expect setbacks to come your way and treat them as potential opportunities to learn from.

Now, it is time for us to look into some practical exercises that will not only help you reinforce all that you have learned, but they will actually help you experience the difference and the results that you have waited for. In the next chapter, we will look into some of my most favorite methods that have genuinely helped me gain mental toughness and become a better person. Get ready to experience something new, something exciting and something that you can use every day for the rest of your life.

Chapter 6

Building on Mental Toughness in Five Minutes a Day

With just five minutes every day, you can build upon your mental toughness right away. The best news is that there is no hidden catch here either. You do not have to invest your finances or do insanely difficult exercises to get the results. What you are about to read is extremely simple, and it can be done anywhere, anytime, and by anyone. The results are almost instant but they last for a significantly long time. Welcome then to the world of meditation - the exercise that changed everything for me!

Meditation - The Game Changer

Let me start by asking you a very simple question. How do you build your body and make it physically stronger? You hit the gym and work out for months. The eventual result, provided that you also do what is required outside of the gym, is a stronger looking body. We know how to train our muscles and make them stronger, but what about our mind? How can we train our mental state to grow stronger and gain the kind of mental toughness it needs to move forward? Well, that's where meditation comes in.

For anyone who may not have heard about meditation, let me give you an introductory class. Meditation is considered as the most effective way to reduce and manage stress and anxiety. It is one of the finest ways to help build mental toughness because through mediation, you gain the ability to focus on what truly matters to you while discarding any other thought as if it didn't exist.

According to Mayo Clinic, a renowned organization, meditation has been around for a very, very long time. It has been practiced for thousands of years. While it was initially introduced as a method to connect with the spiritual self, it soon adopted a different purpose. Today, meditation is one of the most commonly used methods for relaxation and controlling stress of any kind (Mayo Clinic, n.d.).

I use meditation every single day not only because it helps me develop further upon my mental toughness, but it greatly helps me in wiping away all the stress that I may have. It is one way to gain inner peace. It is true. What makes meditation truly unique is how easy it is to use and master.

You only need to spend a few minutes and you will experience results like none other. No other technique that I know of can provide you with a mental relief the way meditation can. Whether you are anxious about a situation, tense, or even worried, meditation can help you get your flow back. It can help you focus your energy to solutions while throwing away your problems. So what exactly is meditation then? How does it work?

Meditation is essentially a mind-body complementary medicine. It is an exercise that helps you create a "deep state of relaxation and a tranquil mind." (Mayo Clinic, n.d.). Of course, if you have such a mental state, making decisions, taking risks, and solving problems become a lot easier.

Our mind is processing millions of bits of information every second. That is a massive number. This means that our mind is constantly occupied with something, and that is what often makes us feel like we have far too much going on in our head. It is usually at this point that we start experiencing anxiety and stress building. The more these two build up, the more compromised our mental state becomes. By introducing meditation to the mix, we have an opportunity to level the playing field and gain back our optimum thinking capacity.

There are many, and I repeat, many benefits that mediation can bring to you, all within a few minutes of your time. Here are some that I have personally experienced even today:

- Helps gain new perspective on matters
- Builds the much-needed skills to effectively manage stress
- Allows us to focus on the present
- Increases our creativity and imagination
- Cuts down on negative emotions
- Increases something called self-awareness
- Increases tolerance and patience significantly

If that isn't enough, here are some more benefits it is possible to experience:

- Controls anxiety
- Boosts emotional health
- Increases concentration spans
- Can possibly reduce the age-related loss of memory (Thorpe, 2020)
- Helps generate kindness
- Fights addictions
- Controls blood pressure (decrease)
- Controls heart rhythm
- Improves sleep
- Greatly helps in controlling pain

You do not need to have special equipment nor do you need to worry about gaining a degree in psychology just so you can reap the benefits of meditation. Anyone can do it, and it is completely pain free.

Athletes around the world use meditation to regain their strength, increase their mental toughness and reflexes. It helps them focus more on the present and stop worrying about "what if" and "what could've been." This paves way for them to commit to what they focus on.

Meditation In Action

Meditation isn't something that people claim to be effective. There has been significant research that has been carried out to find out if meditation is as good as people claim it to be. One particular research involved six national swimmers between the ages of fourteen and seventeen. A pre-test of mental toughness was conducted and their average score was 3.2. The total score was 38.12. Their problem-solving scores were 96.25 before the research began. Remember, for problem-solving scores, the higher the number, the weaker the problem-solving ability.

These swimmers were tasked to practice meditation for the next twelve weeks. Throughout these twelve weeks, these swimmers continued with their routine activities and only added meditation to their routine. Once the twelve weeks ended, they were put through the same tests again. This time, however, the scores were beyond extraordinary. Their mental toughness score average shot up to 4.1, or a total of 45.37. That is a remarkable 15% leap in just as little as twelve weeks. Their problem-solving scores improved as well as they now managed to score 78.25, and that equates to an improvement of 16%.

The research concluded that meditation is a powerful mental training tool that can help future athletes break records after records. This research also concluded that meditation lives up to its name and reputation because the data clearly suggests that meditation can not only improve mental health, but it can also go on to improve physical performances as well (Ekmekçi & Miçooğulları, 2019).

Types of Meditation

There are many types of meditation for you to choose from. Each of these types will allow you to gain and experience almost the same results with only a difference of mechanism. It is also worth noticing that some of these techniques involve moving around while others may require you to remain still and relaxed. Some of these techniques work great in a quiet environment, however, if you are someone who is always on the move, rest assured that there are ways you can also take benefit of meditation. I will explain each of these techniques and how they work.

Guided Meditation

One of the most common types of meditation is called the guided meditation. As the name implies, this type of meditation involves having a guide that can direct you through the process, tell you when to breathe in and out, sit, lie down, stand, imagine and visualize. This type of meditation is great for a person or a group of people who prefer having someone else guide them.

It is also a good idea to use some free demo guided meditation sessions online. You can browse millions of guided meditation videos online and use these to practice meditation. Once you get the idea of how things work, you can then arrange a group activity or start meditating on your own without the help of guides.

The guided meditation is one that helps you get in touch with all your senses. Through a technique called visualization, which is essentially visualizing the scene within your mind, you can use your senses one by one, and grow more self-aware of your surroundings. It is also an exploratory experience that helps you to reduce stress and feel rejuvenated and reenergized once again.

Mantra Meditation

You may have seen this type of meditation in movies and films. This is the type of meditation where one sits in a comfortable posture, whatever it may be, and then focuses his thoughts and energy on words or phrases that they continue to repeat. Words such as "Om" or "Inner peace" are popularly used by many.

This type of meditation helps you develop your focusing skills and helps you to focus on a single sound or thought. Wherever you feel your mind is wandering away, you repeat the phrase or mantra and bring your focus back.

With that said, this type of meditation is best experienced in silence and isolation. You cannot expect to meditate and focus uninterruptedly in crowded places or places that may have a lot of noise.

Mindfulness Meditation

Do not be intimidated with the term "mindfulness." It is nothing more than a state where one is completely aware of whatever exists in the present and accepts whatever goes on to live in the present moment. However, despite it sounding so simple and plain, the benefits of this meditation go far beyond what words can define.

Through mindfulness meditation, you allow your consciousness to broaden up. In this exercise, you focus your energy on the natural flow of your breath. Whatever thoughts that may come, you are to let them pass without passing any judgment. By doing so, you will gain the ability to focus more on the present without worrying about being distracted by other thoughts that may have nothing to do with the present.

Qi Gong

This is a kind of traditional Chinese medicine. The technique involves a combination of basic meditation, physical movement, relaxation and some breathing exercises. All of these combined are done to restore balance within a person.

Yoga

This is arguably the most famous type of meditation in existence today. This type of meditation involves you to perform a variety of postures. Furthermore, you are required to exercise controlled breathing to help promote the body to be more flexible. It is also a great way to calm your mind when you have had a very stressful day.

With yoga, however, you must always consult your doctor if you have underlying conditions as some postures can exert pressure or cause discomfort to people suffering from ailments. Be sure to get a go ahead before performing yoga.

The poses you acquire and maintain while controlling your breath, you will use balance and concentration as some of these poses can often be tricky to maintain and hold. By doing so, you will eventually start focusing all your energy on that moment and forgetting about everything else, which is why those who do yoga end the session feeling rejuvenated.

Important Aspects of Meditation

There are quite a few components that one should familiarize themselves with in order to extract the best results from meditation every single time. While each type of meditation may involve additional features that help you meditate, most of these components remain the same.

Focused Attention

One of the most important aspects about meditation is to use your ability to focus. Even if you lack concentration in the start, you will learn how to increase your concentration span with a few exercises. You can start by focusing on your breathing pattern or visualizing yourself as seen from somebody else's eye. Whatever works for you, use that to maintain focus. Where you feel like your mind is wandering off, realign your focus accordingly.

For me, I started focusing on my count from zero to 100. Breathe in, count one, breathe out, count the next number, and continue moving on. Focus on the number itself to help you concentrate.

Breathe Easy

There is no reason to breathe in rapidly or extremely slowly. Meditation isn't a sport that requires you to increase your lung capacity. Breathe naturally as you normally would. Some exercises, however, may require you to breathe a little slower than usual, but even that is acceptable. Whatever feels normal and relaxing for you, stick with that. Your breathing should be evenly paced. Once you are in a flow, slow your breathing down slightly to allow more oxygen to reach your lungs. It also helps you to relax your shoulders, chest and neck as slow and deliberate breathing reduces the use of these parts of the body allowing a more efficient breathing experience.

Quiet is Good

There is no denying that the best experiences are the ones that are experienced in quieter settings. There is something unique, something different about how the experience feels like when you do it right. While Qi Gong and some other exercises involve you to move about, often following someone else's voice, the meditation you do on your own in a quiet setting is just phenomenal. You feel more focused, energized, and motivated. You are able to easily observe the chain of thought and let them go out of your brain without being judgemental. Besides, some may feel comfortable meditating alone as opposed to being in the presence of others.

Once you are able to master this technique, you will be able to practice this even within your office because by then, you would have mastered the ability to maintain focus even in high stress and pressure situations.

Comfortable Position

To make the best of the meditation session, you must ensure that you practice meditation in a comfortable position. Find a place that provides you with an option to be seated comfortably or even lie down if you wish to. The more comfortable you are when beginning to meditate, the better the results will be.

Open Mind

Allow yourself to have an open mind. Whatever thought that may come to your mind, you must not tie any emotions to it, and allow any such thought to pass through without the need of passing a judgment, even if it is something you truly hate. By doing so, you empty your mind and clear away the clutter of thoughts that are otherwise preoccupied in creating stress.

How to Meditate

Now that you know the basic concepts and all the important bits about meditation, it is time to start learning some extremely easy and interesting methods to mediate your stress and worries away. If you missed out the previous part about the important components that go into making a meditation session a successful one, I recommend you to browse back and read through these aspects before proceeding.

Breathing Deeply

This is perhaps the easiest one of the lot. It literally requires no special postures or any movement of any kind making it the perfect method for beginners. All you need is to find yourself a suitable place to sit or lie down. Ensure that the place you are meditating is away from noise and distractions, such as TV or cell phones.

Once you have found a comfortable place and position, start by breathing in deeply and exhaling slowly. As you breathe in, focus on how the air enters your nose, goes through your system and into the lungs. Feel the chest expanding as air flows in. Listen to the sound you are making when inhaling and exhaling. Then, exhale and do the same. Feel the chest contract as the air is pushed out through your mouth. For the next few minutes, continue doing this. If you feel like you are having intruding thoughts, refocus on your breathing experience. Ideally, you should continue doing this with eyes closed and for at least five to ten minutes. Once done, slowly breathe in and exhale, and as you do so, open your eyes slowly to end the session.

I will not tell you what you will feel. I leave that part for you to experience on your own. If you do not feel better, lighter and slightly happier, you either got distracted or you did not meditate correctly.

Scanning the Body

This method uses pretty much the same setting with one major difference. This time, instead of focusing our mind on our breathing, we tend to focus on our body and scan it. Think about it like having a camera that is facing you and starts at the very top of your head. As you breathe in and out slowly, it starts to go down. Visualize every part of the body as the point of focus moves down. Try and feel the muscles of that particular region. If you find your muscles are stiff, try and relax them without opening your eyes or moving much. If your neck is stiff, move your neck a little to relax and release muscle tension. Continue doing the same all the way to the tip of your toe. Once done, go back up to the top of your head to scan your body all the way through.

This generally takes anywhere between five to ten minutes. For beginners, this may take up to fifteen minutes at times as well. The idea isn't to pace through but to create an experience that rejuvenates the mind and body. Through this exercise, you familiarize yourself with every muscle of your body and learn to feel what pain, relaxation, warmth and tension feels like. After mastering this ability, you will soon gain the ability to know right away which part of your body is stiff, which we normally are told by the doctors. Most of the time, you can then meditate and relax your muscles right away, giving you back all the time and energy to get the job done.

Walk and Meditate

This one is certainly different, but that does not mean this doesn't work or that it produces lesser results. There are those who prefer to meditate and up their physical health as well. This is a great way to do so. The best thing about this kind of meditation is that you can use it virtually anywhere and in any kind of situation that involves walking.

You start by slowing down your walking pace so that you are able to easily focus your energy on each movement and step that you take. Ensure that you do not focus on a destination, such as where your foot may land. Focus on your legs and feet and as you move, repeat the words "moving," "lifting," and "placing" to match the action that is being taken at that point in time. Continue doing this for as long as you intend to walk. Once again, if your mind wanders off, which it easily can, bring your attention back to your legs and feet to maintain concentration.

These are three of my favorite techniques that I personally use along with visualization. By visualizing the scenes, such as a relaxing day out on the beach, all alone by myself, with cool air breezing past and the warm sun shining down upon me, I find it a lot easier to remain in that zone for a while before ending the meditation session. You can try your hand with visualization too as it certainly helps you boost your creativity and imagination, bringing to life new sensations as you push your senses to be active and experience the visualization as if it was real. The experience, therefore, is second to none.

Now that you have all you need to get started with meditation, make it a routine to meditate everyday. I meditate twice a day, once in the morning before I start my work, and once after returning home from a hard day's work. This allows me to ensure I walk into my workplace with a fresh and open mind, and come back home feeling relaxed and calm. You can meditate as many times as you want to, however, it is generally observed that these two times are well-suited to most.

With that said, it is now time to take things up a notch and learn ten extremely easy steps you can take to build upon your mental toughness starting now.

Chapter 7:

Ten Easy Steps to Build

Mental Toughness

I am sure that a lot of you were astonished by the results meditation was able to provide you. Hopefully, you must now be able to understand why I love meditating. It certainly does help me when things aren't easy or when the going gets rough. It helps me calm my mind, gather my thoughts and regain the energy and focus I need to exercise my mental toughness and move on. However, it would be wrong of me to say that meditation is the only thing that helps me to move ahead.

Therefore, in this chapter, I will share with you ten very easy steps that you can take to further build upon your mental toughness. These are the very same steps I took when I was starting to explore the concept of mental toughness. They certainly helped me and everyone else that I shared these steps with, which is why I am very confident that they will help you feel the difference as well.

The Ten Steps

It took me years to figure these steps out and learn them before I was anywhere close to applying them into my life. Fortunately for you, you do not have to spend years searching for these. Through these ten steps, you get to build your mental toughness and take it to the next level. Consider these as a step-by-step guide to help you move in the right direction and gain the kind of mental toughness you have been seeking all this time. Each of these steps are essentially things that you will need to practice on and remember for the rest of your life. You can apply these in virtually all aspects of life.

Step One - Push the Boundary

Start by doing whatever you do to make yourself physically healthy. If you are someone who goes to the gym and does ten reps every set, push yourself for the eleventh the next time you are around. There is no point in doing something over and over again just because it is comfortable. To develop mental toughness, let go of your comfort zone and push yourself further than what you think is possible. It is just a single rep, but the results will be far more worthy.

"The secret is to go one small step beyond what you mentally believe you can do." (Denning, 2018)

With each passing day, do something more than you would normally do. If you drink five glasses of water, add another one. If you wake up by six in the morning, try and wake up thirty minutes earlier. The more you do for your physical body, the easier it will be to develop mental toughness. The principle is simple, the tougher we are, the longer we can endure and go.

Step Two - Knowing Things Will Go Wrong

Okay, this isn't exactly the kind of motivation you need, but to be mentally tough, you must start preparing your mind for a situation that could happen well before time. It is easy to find yourself slightly confused or, at worse, completely baffled when things may not turn out the way you were hoping for. To avoid that, start by telling yourself that things are bound to go wrong.

Once your mind accepts that, only then can you prepare it for the worst outcome. Only then can you exercise your mental toughness and develop the kind of focus and energy you need to deal with such a situation that may or may not arise at all.

If you are someone who prefers to remain a perfectionist, know that perfection is a recipe for disaster. If everything goes perfectly, there is no room for you to exercise your mental toughness in, meaning that you will eventually start losing your mental toughness with time. It also means that soon, you will be deviating from the path you intended to pursue. Always expect some kind of failure or obstacle to come in your way.

Step Three - Catch Some Z's

Negative thoughts or emotions are bound to arrive, even to someone with extremely high mental toughness. It is a natural part of life and there is no way that can help you avoid these. Since these are inevitable, we might as well learn how to deal with them. One great way is to sleep all your negative emotions and feelings off. By doing so, you will wake up feeling a thousand times better than what you might have felt had you chosen to stay up and ponder upon these results or emotions.

The problem with negative emotions is that they can often lure you into an emotional trap. If that happens, you may not react in an emotionally healthy manner, hence messing the situation up badly. Once you take these negative emotions to bed and tell yourself that you will tend to these the next day, you are putting aside all your emotional impulses and outbursts. The next day, even if the problem remains, you will have gained significant mental toughness to handle things in a far more productive manner. There will be no outburst or yelling or screaming at all, and that is a good thing.

Step Four - Hello Brightside

There is always a bright side to things, whether we like to admit it or not. Even if we fail to achieve something after years of hard work and dedication, there is still a ray of hope, a brighter side to things. All you need is to keep an open mind and seek out the bright side.

If you were unable to buy yourself a house this year, it is possible that you might have bought the same house at a higher price. It is also possible that the house might have been too expensive to maintain and would have pushed you around in all sorts of trouble. It is also possible the fact you do not end up buying saves you a chunk of money which you can then use to reinvest in business and make even more profits. Do not rush into analyzing the negative aspects of the situation. Always try and seek out the positives first. If it helps, seek assistance to gain a new perspective on things and find out what you might not be able to see due to your emotions clouding your thought process.

Step Five - Goals Over Dreams

I may dream of being a president, but that is certainly not my goal. I may dream of driving my own Lamborghini, but that is certainly not what I intend to work for. My goals and my dreams are two separate entities, two separate ideas. They are neither interlinked nor do they share the same path I choose to pursue. By knowing the difference between the two, it makes it easier to focus more on my goal as opposed to my dream because I know, with time, my dreams will keep changing but my goals will remain constant.

Whatever goals you set for yourself, they always take priority. I am not suggesting that you give up on your dreams, but wait for them until you have achieved your goals. A goal is something that is clearly defined and laid out using a solid plan. It is something that requires a person to do their homework before they are able to even begin working towards it. For mental toughness to shine through, you must define your goals as clearly as possible, and for good reasons too.

Our mind accepts and works upon whatever is clearly defined. Anything that may have vagueness or confusion or contradiction, it will discard or ignore said ideas right away. Sure, you can force your mind to work for you, but it will not be doing so at an optimum level. Think about your school days and the assignments you had to do. Since they were hard and not defined well, you would yawn every chance you'd get, indicating that your mind was not collaborating with you. On the other hand, if you were working on something that was in line with your interests, goals, and vision, you would hardly remember a yawn other than the one that indicated you were tired because with such assignments, you were clearly interested.

Always focus on the goals as opposed to your dreams. Goals are far easier to achieve, are clearly laid out in plans, and are easily breakable into smaller, more achievable pieces.

Step Six - Accept Pain

There is no easy way to put this so I will be as straightforward as possible. If you wish to be successful, wealthy, famous, and go on to achieve your goals, you must accept pain as a part of your life. Whether it is the pain of losing something, failing at your tasks, or even a physical one, tell yourself that it's a part of what you are trying to do. Sure, you do have the option of avoiding it, but if you are trying to be mentally tough, it is practically impossible to do that.

Step Seven - Bye Bye Comfort Zone

I have already spoken about this earlier, which is why I am fairly confident that you already know what you must do.

Start breaking your comfort zone by doing the opposite of what makes you comfortable. If you prefer taking a shower with hot water in the morning, turn the cold water tap on instead. Let your body experience the new changes and adapt to them. This will allow you to not only gain superior physical and mental strength but it will also help you gain mental toughness.

Step Eight - Easy on the Mind

When we encounter negative emotions, our mind starts depleting its energy twice as fast. What we must understand is that our mind, just like any traditional car, has a limited supply of fuel (energy). When it runs out, it stops functioning properly.

Quite often, we end up using our horn to show our displeasure when someone isn't moving or moving slowly. It is highly unlikely that using the horn would change anything. It isn't that the other person would come out and apologize. This means we wasted our energy towards a negative emotion. What we should actually be doing instead is something quite hard; remain calm. Of course, it is easier said than done, but by doing so, you are preserving the fuel and disciplining yourself and your mind.

Mental toughness does not grant you a license to do anything that harms others. Instead, use your energy and mental toughness to inspire yourself to move forward and do a good job. You can couple this with any other personal development technique you may have picked up. You can always top up on your mental energy by consuming the proper nutrients your body needs. Do that and you can go the entire day without ever running out of energy.

Step Nine - Prepare Your Mind

When you are met with a situation that you or your mind have never experienced before, it is likely that you may feel overwhelmed and fail. However, if you encounter something that you already know, are familiar with and are prepared for, there is every chance that you would know what needs to be done.

In a much similar fashion, whatever your goals may be, whatever you may set out to achieve, prepare your mind accordingly. A prepared mind finds success more easily than a mind that isn't prepared.

"The mind becomes weak when it's required to perform at an extraordinary level and has never had to endure this type of struggle before." (Denning, 2018)

If you want a simpler explanation, here is one that will make sense right away. To enter a weightlifting competition, you must first train your muscles to be able to lift the weight.

Step 10 - Keep Distractions at Bay

From our televisions to our cell phones, everything that doesn't directly serve you a purpose is a noise, and any kind of noise is a distraction. Although mental toughness teaches you how to remain focused, and meditation does a fairly good job alone, it is still easy to find yourself distracted. At times, distraction can cause you to suffer significant losses, the likes of which cannot be withstood.

Get rid of all the distractions, especially when you are in the zone, pacing through your tasks. You need all your focus, energy and concentration to get the job done in time and without compromising your quality. Do not allow yourself to be at the mercy of these distractions as they can genuinely throw you off the course and into something that is completely unacceptable to you.

With that said, these are ten steps you can start taking right now and repeat every day. These steps will allow you to evolve into a more mentally tough person. Complement your new personality with meditation and exercises, and watch how your complete lifestyle changes right before your eyes.

In the next chapter, we will look into how we can use mental toughness to achieve our goals.

Chapter 8:

How to Achieve Goals with Mental Toughness

Here is an interesting fact for you to know. Around 80% of the people never even set goals in their lives. Surprisingly enough, of the 20% who find and set their goals, 70% of the people miraculously fail to achieve said goals. You might be thinking that they did not set easy, small or even achievable goals, but they actually did, and yet, they failed to achieve these (Vermeeren, n.d.).

The reason that happens is because these 70% of the people are missing out on mental toughness. They may acquire the skill but they never tend to use it. By not doing so, they expose themselves to a variety of reasons that eventually lead them to failure. In this chapter, we will be looking at some of these aspects and learn why these people fail to achieve goals. Once that is done, we will then look into what we can do to ensure we don't end up in the same situation.

Why Do People Fail?

While there may be a lot more reasons than the ones I list down here, the ones below are the most common ones that I have found throughout my research.

1. **Fearing failure or success -** Although the fear of failure is quite common, there exists what is known as fear of success. People often stop halfway through because they undermine their own abilities, fearing that they are bound to fail. On the other hand, we have people who are far too worried and frightened about what will happen if they succeed. They have no idea what they will do next, and that idea alone terrifies them. With such a mindset, a person is bound to meet failure.

2. **Lack of understanding -** People may find the courage to set goals, but they do not take the time out to fully research and understand the goal itself. They may want to set up a business, but just saying so does not mean it's a goal worth chasing. There are far too many variables involved, a lot of planning that goes into it, and strategies that need to be implemented. Most do not actually do their homework, and that leads them to an inevitable failure that awaits them right at the start of their journey.

3. **Lacking commitment -** Every goal, regardless of how small or big it may be, requires a person to have 100% commitment. There is no such thing as "90%" or even "99%" in the process. If you are committed to a goal, you must be fully committed. Allowing yourself a room of even a single percent would eventually make you weak and lazy, leading you to believe that it is okay to take things easily. While you do that, someone else will jump ahead of you and go on to steal your goal from right under your nose. You must always be at the top of your game and be 100% committed every single day.

4. **Not being active -** Some people tend to stop midway because they think they have come a long way, and that they have achieved some of the goal, if not most of it. Do not allow yourself to fall for this trap. This will essentially push you to lose your commitment level, and we all know what happens if you start compromising on commitment.

5. **Bogged down with questions -** Whatever goal you set, you will find many questions. However, this does not mean that you should have answers to all of these questions. You are not perfect and nor are you supposed to have answers to all "what if" questions. It is natural to have some questions that are left unanswered

or answered by someone else who may excel in that area. Do not waste your time finding answers first and then start. Instead, know the answers to some and get started. You will still have plenty of time to learn in the future. Who knows that the questions you may have might be answered with time automatically.

6. **Having no real destination** - Your goal must be one that defines what you truly wish to become or achieve by the end of said goal. Earlier in the book, I talked at length about setting SMART goals. A lot of people set goals that are not specific because they fail to define a destination. If you do that, you are bound to end up as a failure because you will never know where you are supposed to go and how far off you are from your goal. Always set goals that define a clear destination.

7. **No concrete plan** - Planning is the most important aspect of chasing success. You can be as mentally tough as you prefer to be, but if you do not have a rock-solid plan, you will never be able to use any of your mental toughness or other skills. Always plan well ahead of time and know what you are supposed to do, by when, and how. After that, let your mental toughness do the rest for you as you go out ensuring that these tasks and goals are brought to fruition.

8. **Bombarded by goals** - A lot of people fail because they often end up having a lot more on their plate than they can handle. In this case, they gather so many plans that they lose track of what they are doing and where they are supposed to go. Focus on a single plan, bring it into motion and achieve it before moving on to the next one. For short-term goals, you can have a few plans lined up, but it is generally preferred that you handle one goal at a time to ensure your focus is always 100% and not divided.

9. **Feeling unworthy** - No one is born unworthy, everyone is born equal. Despite that, there are many who still believe that they do not deserve to achieve such a massive success that they end their run even before it begins. Once again, they are failing to achieve what could possibly become a game-changer for them in life. If you are someone who feels that way, meditation is a great way to come out of your negative emotions. Add to that your mental toughness, and you are all set to go out there and conquer the challenges.

10. **Lacking motivation to change matters** - Change is a universal constant. While everything on earth is unpredictable, change isn't. Every second brings change, whether small or big.

People often fear changes because they believe that these may throw them off their course or change how things usually work. Once again, they have created for themselves a comfort zone. To be successful, one must accept change as an opportunity, and should be willing to step out of their comfort zone to truly pursue success.

I am sure you have already figured out on how you can go on to achieve your goals using mental toughness. The answers are to do exactly the opposite of what I have highlighted in bold letters above. However, to ensure that everyone understands, let me quickly explain what you need to do in order to achieve your goals with mental toughness that you have worked hard for.

Set Clear Goals

Your goals must be crystal clear. They should be well thought of and well defined. Goals usually work best when they are aligned with your passion and interests. Anything outside of these may prove to be too difficult to pursue. Your goals must be the kind of goals that encourage you to change things around, be more active and go out of your comfort zone to pursue said goals.

Have Motivation and Self-Discipline

Earlier in the book, I spoke on how self-discipline helps you correct your errors and keeps you at the top of your game, especially when the odds are stacking up against you. However, self-discipline alone may not get the job done. To fill in the gap, you also need motivation. I find it very motivating to have little reminders on my cell phone or work stations that use only a few words to show what my goals are. You can use any mechanism that, when referred to, instills you with a sense of confidence. Your self-discipline will ensure that you follow a healthy routine and do everything right, allowing you more motivation. Add to that these little hacks, your motivation will be through the roof. Literally nothing will stand between you and your goals.

Give it Your Best Shot, Everyday

Here is a simple one-liner tip for you: Every day, bring in 100% commitment, no ifs or buts.

Endure and Tolerate

A lot of things may not go the way you planned. You may have to work with people you might not really like. However, all of that is okay. You should develop endurance and tolerance within you to accept whatever is going on and still remain focused on your eventual goals. Whatever the mechanism, whatever the setting, you must not break character nor get involved into something that pushes you away from your goal because the second you move away, it will virtually be impossible to get back on track and make up for the lost time. Time is a valuable asset that cannot be bought or sold. Therefore, do not waste it.

Be Realistic

Your goals and your actions must be realistic in nature. There is no point in putting in efforts to do something that is completely unrealistic. Use the SMART goals tool to help you set realistic goals and tasks. Anything that falls outside of that must be discarded. Always consider what resources you have, what you can do, and what your limitations are. Do not attempt to do something that demands you more than what you can offer.

Hold Yourself Accountable

Whatever actions you take, know that you will be accountable for them. Whether the results come out positive or otherwise, do not shy away from taking responsibility as doing so will literally obliterate your mental toughness. Even if you are the owner of an organization, you are still to be held accountable, meaning that you may need to explain why you took certain steps to those who may be working for you or are in important positions within the organization.

Hopefully, you noted these down somewhere for future reference. Consider these are ingredients for a recipe that helps you create mental toughness for yourself. Up until now, we have learned everything about mental toughness. All that remains now is to learn how we can ensure we maintain mental toughness for the rest of our lives, and that's what our next chapter will talk about.

Chapter 9:

How to Maintain Being Mentally Tough

Firstly, congratulations on making it this far. Now, you know what it takes to be mentally tough. However, it is now time to understand what we need to do in order to remain mentally tough. Trust me, it is fairly easy to lose mental toughness over the course of time, and I am not even talking about years. If you do not continue doing what needs to be done for a few weeks, your mental toughness will take a nose-dive.

Therefore, this chapter will talk about what you need to do to maintain your mental toughness for years to come.

Retaining Mental Toughness

Perhaps the most obvious answer is to continue doing what we have learned so far. Frankly, that is correct. Sometimes, the answers that seem too obvious are actually the right ones. In this case, consistency is the answer you are looking for.

Whatever we have learned so far, it is consistency that keeps the momentum going forward. You start today, and a year down the road, you will have a momentum that has kept on building for 365 days. Miss out a single day and you immediately break the momentum. When you break the momentum for a single day, you allow your subconscious to know that it is okay to take a break at times. Next time, whether you like it or not, you will start skipping on days, eventually missing out the entire year.

Once you start with mental toughness, know that it is a one-way ticket. You cannot expect to stop whenever or wherever you want to. You must continue with the momentum for the rest of your life if you are to truly experience life-altering results.

A lot of people often end up completing a few goals and achieving success in a few years. They then go on to hire people to get most of their jobs done for them, and at this point, they start taking things easy because they believe they have earned it. You can never earn to sit back, relax and chill out because the second you do that, you are practically saying goodbye to your future potential success. If you genuinely wish to be a success story that people go on to talk about, you must never stop. Why do I say that? You, being a leader of the company, represent what the company is all about. If you start taking things slowly and easily, others will follow your footsteps. Laying off people isn't the answer either because if you do so, you might be in for some legal complications. Truly then, the only option you have is to carry on with the momentum and give everyday your max. To help you keep the momentum alive, here are five great methods I learned and used to keep me going.

Start Small, Start Simple

Whatever tasks you may have for any given day, break them down into smaller pieces. Start with the simplest ones first and get these sorted right away. Start moving towards the tougher ones, and accomplish these one by one. Before you know it, you would have created a mini-momentum that keeps you going towards the end of your day. This momentum will always ensure that you carry on doing what you are supposed to do every single day without compromising or missing out on your momentum.

Reward Yourself on Progress

Self-assurance and self-praise are mighty tools. When you get a job done, reward yourself by praising how good a job you have done. It also helps if you can celebrate your smaller wins. Despite the tasks being small, celebrating their completion plays to your psychological advantage. It keeps you motivated, knowing that you have done your tasks, regardless of their size or complexity.

Whenever you walk into your office or workplace, always ensure that you reward yourself in some way or celebrate the smaller achievements to keep the momentum going and your mind charged with motivation.

Share

This may sound a little strange, but if you share your goal or vision with a partner, you then create a system that always pushes you to do your best. Your partner, just like you, will also be held accountable for their actions, but this will always ensure that you and your partner put your efforts together to accomplish goals that might have been too much for you to handle. Hold yourself accountable by sharing your progress and vice versa. Help each other out by providing constructive feedback and praising each other on a job well done.

Know Your Purpose

Whatever goals you may have, ask yourself why you intend to seek them. Whatever the answer is, that is your purpose. The more exciting the purpose, the more eager and motivated you will be to achieve said goals.

Reverse-Gap Thinking

Almost everyone is fixated on how far they have to go in life. I use what is called reverse-gap thinking. When I look upon my goals, I think about how far I have come, and that perspective allows me to fill myself up with pride, happiness and a sense of accomplishment.

Having positive feelings is always a plus, and now, I have just shared with you a simple yet powerful way to look upon your goals. By knowing how far you have come in life, you will always find reasons to smile, to feel motivated and happy. These emotions alone are enough to keep the momentum going for the rest of your life.

Put all of these together, and what you end up is a perpetual supply of fuel for your momentum to use. For as long as you continue doing these, your momentum will never come to a halt. Your momentum is far more powerful than you might imagine. If you do not believe me, look at how far we have come. You started with a book that you knew not what it would teach, and now we are parting ways after sharing significant knowledge and experiences. Take a moment now to pause, take a deep breath, and pat yourself on the back. You have just proved to yourself that you have what it takes to be mentally tough and keep that momentum going.

Conclusion

We started on a journey to learn what mental toughness is all about. Frankly, there were a lot of questions, confusions, and rightfully so. We are not taught what mental toughness is and why it is important to have it. The only way we get to know about its existence is if someone else talks about it, or we start exploring answers to questions no one else can answer. Whatever it was that brought you here, congratulations. Not only did you learn what mental toughness is, but you also got to learn how you can build your own from home, without any specialized knowledge, degree or experience.

Throughout the book, I spoke on what mental toughness is, what makes it so popular with athletes, and how people go on to use it in life. I shed light on what it takes to become mentally tough, and what possible benefits you can expect to get once you become mentally tough.

Later, I explained my all-time favourite technique of meditation, a technique as old as time that helps everyone relieve stress, break away anxiety and defeat depression. It is truly a unique way to not only gain mental toughness but also defeat all that stands in the way of us and our success.

Finally, we moved on to some practical aspects of the book where we learned how you can build on mental toughness and how you can maintain mental toughness for the rest of your life. For me, the journey might have ended here, but for you, it has just begun.

There is far too much to learn, experience, and understand in life. As long as you keep an open mind, welcome challenges with positivity and maintain a momentum, there is nothing that can stop you from achieving the impossible. I certainly hope that this book was able to help you out in discovering the amazing world of mental toughness. If it did, I encourage you to leave a positive feedback and let me know what you think. It is through your feedback that I get the confidence to do more. Until next time, stay safe and stay mentally tough!

References

American Sleep Association. (n.d.). *Sleep and Sleep Disorder Statistics*. American Sleep Association. https://www.sleepassociation.org/about-sleep/sleep-statistics/

APA. (2020, October). *Stress in America 2020*. Apa.org. https://www.apa.org/news/press/releases/stress/2020/report-october

Bollinger, A. (2020, November 26). *How to Develop Mental Toughness and Stay Strong*. Lifehack. https://www.lifehack.org/articles/productivity/how-to-develop-mental-toughness.html

Denning, T. (2018, March 24). *Developing Warrior Like Mental Toughness — 11 Easy Steps*. Medium. https://medium.com/startup-grind/developing-warrior-like-mental-toughness-11-easy-steps-c9437ce5fb22

Ekmekçi, R., & Miçooğulları, B. O. (2019). Developing Mental Toughness with Mental Training and Meditation. *PIET-19, ALSH-19, MEIS-19 Oct. 16-18, 2019 Lisbon (Portugal)*. https://doi.org/10.17758/eirai7.dir1019410

Jones, G. (2002). What Is This Thing Called Mental Toughness? An Investigation of Elite Sport Performers. *Journal of Applied Sport Psychology, 14*(3), 205–218. https://doi.org/10.1080/10413200290103509

Lyons, P. (n.d.). *What Is The Difference Between Resilience and Mental Toughness?* The Outperformer; The Outperformer. https://www.theoutperformer.co/post/what-is-the-difference-between-resilience-and-mental-toughness-paul-lyons

Mayo Clinic. (n.d.). *Meditation: A simple, fast way to reduce stress.* Mayo Clinic. https://www.mayoclinic.org/tests-procedures/meditation/in-depth/meditation/art-20045858

Mental Toughness Inc. (n.d.). *What is mental toughness?* https://www.mentaltoughnessinc.com/what-is-mental-toughness/

Mental Toughness Partners. (n.d.). *You Can Measure Mental Toughness.* Www.Mentaltoughness.Partners. Retrieved December 27, 2020, from https://www.mentaltoughness.partners/measure-mental-toughness/

SLMA. (n.d.). *The Science of STRESS.* SLMA. https://www.slma.cc/the-science-of-stress/

Sutton, J. (2019, September 5). *What Is Mental Toughness, and Where Can I Get Some?* Medium. https://elemental.medium.com/what-is-mental-toughness-and-where-can-i-get-some-e1e2ae902cf4

The Times. (n.d.). *The Sunday Times Rich List 2020.* Www.Thetimes.co.uk. Retrieved December 25, 2020, from https://www.thetimes.co.uk/sunday-times-rich-list

Thorpe, M. (2020, October 27). *12 Science-Based Benefits of Meditation.* Healthline. https://www.healthline.com/nutrition/12-benefits-of-meditation#5.-Lengthens-attention-span

Vermeeren, D. (n.d.). *Why People Fail to Achieve Their Goals.* Reliableplant.com; Noria Corporation. https://www.reliableplant.com/Read/8259/fail-achieve-goals

Vulliamy, E. (2015, December 17). *11 ways to become a mentally strong person.* The Independent. https://www.independent.co.uk/news/11-ways-become-mentally-strong-person-a6776641.html

Williams, C. (2017, September 25). *Five ways science can improve your focus.* Www.Bbc.com. https://www.bbc.com/worklife/article/201709

25-the-surprising-tricks-to-help-you-focus-at-work